COOKIES

COOKIES

150 DELICIOUS COOKIES, BROWNIES, BARS AND BISCUITS SHOWN IN 270 INSPIRATIONAL PHOTOGRAPHS

CATHERINE ATKINSON

WITH RECIPES BY VALERIE BARRETT AND JOANNA FARROW

southwater

This edition is published by Southwater
an imprint of Anness Publishing Ltd
108 Great Russell Street
London WC1B 3NA
info@anness.com

www.southwaterbooks.com
www.annesspublishing.com

If you like the images in this book and would like to investigate using them for publishing, promotions
or advertising, please visit our website www.practicalpictures.com for more information.

A CIP catalogue record for this book is available from the British Library.

Publisher: Joanna Lorenz
Editor: Amy Christian
Recipes: Valerie Barrett and Joanna Farrow
Photography: Craig Robertson and Frank Adam
Production Controller: Pirong Wang

Designed and edited for Anness Publishing Ltd by
the Bridgewater Book Company Ltd

NOTES

Bracketed terms are intended for American readers.
For all recipes, quantities are given in both metric and imperial measures and, where appropriate, in standard cups and spoons.
Follow one set of measures, but not a mixture, because they are not interchangeable.
Standard spoon and cup measures are level. 1 tsp = 5ml, 1 tbsp = 15ml, 1 cup = 250ml/8fl oz.
Australian standard tablespoons are 20ml. Australian readers should use 3 tsp in place of 1 tbsp for measuring small quantities.
American pints are 16fl oz/2 cups. American readers should use 20fl oz/2.5 cups in place of 1 pint when measuring liquids.
Electric oven temperatures in this book are for conventional ovens. When using a fan oven, the temperature will probably need to be reduced
by about 10–20°C/20–40°F. Since ovens vary, you should check with your manufacturer's instruction book for guidance.
The nutritional analysis given for each recipe is calculated per portion (i.e. serving or item), unless otherwise stated. If the recipe gives a range,
such as Serves 4–6, then the nutritional analysis will be for the smaller portion size, i.e. 6 servings. The analysis does not include optional
ingredients, such as salt added to taste.
Medium (US large) eggs are used unless otherwise stated.
Front cover shows Spicy Hearts and Stars – for recipe, see page 68

PUBLISHER'S NOTE

Contents

Introduction

No matter what age you are, a freshly baked cookie is always something to be enjoyed. They are one of the tastiest treats, and what's more they're so simple to make. Cookies, in one form or another, have been around for centuries and some of the most popular cookies today derive from these original recipes.

AN AMERICAN INVENTION

The term cookie was first used in the United States when early Dutch settlers brought their *koekje* (little cakes) to New York. At about the same time, wood-burning and coal-fired ovens were introduced, which made baking much more reliable and the popularity of cookies soon spread throughout the country.

Eastern European, Scandinavian and British immigrants who settled in the United States all added to the cookie-making tradition. For example, refrigerator cookies originated from German Heidesand cookies, which are made by shaping dough into long, sausage-shaped rolls, cutting them into thin, round slices and then baking.

In other countries, the meaning of the word cookie varies. In Scotland, a cookie is a sweetened bread bun that is filled with whipped cream or thickly iced. In Britain and France, cookies are commonly known as biscuits, whereas in the United States, the term biscuit is used to describe a large, soft scone.

EARLY COOKIES

There are differences in opinion about the origins of the word biscuit, but whether it is derived from the French *cuit* or from the Latin *biscoctus*, all agree that it means twice-cooked.

Originally, cookies were double-baked. They were browned for a few minutes when the oven was at its hottest, then removed and returned to the oven as it was cooling down. This dried out the cookies so that they kept well – essential in the days before airtight containers were available. At this time, not all cookies were baked; some were fried into wafers.

BELOW: *A plate of freshly baked cookies is always welcome any time of the day.*

ABOVE: *A modern take on fortune cookies containing predictions of the future.*

ABOVE: *Maryland cookies are a very popular type of chocolate chip cookie.*

ABOVE: *Cornflakes coated in chocolate are always a hit with children.*

During the Middle Ages cookies began to improve. Sugar and spices were added to biscuits to make them more palatable and in the late Middle Ages it was discovered that adding beaten egg to biscuit dough made the finished cookie lighter and that ground nuts could be used instead of flour. This led to the creation of meringue, sponge and macaroon cookies.

Cookie mixtures changed significantly in the 18th and 19th centuries. The tradition of frying cookies disappeared – although in parts of Europe, India and the Middle East some cookies are still fried today – and enriched short cakes became popular. These rich doughs still form the basis of many modern cookies.

Although savoury cheese crackers have their origins in medieval times, savoury crackers were not created until the 18th century. These later developed into salted crackers and cocktail savouries for nibbling with drinks.

During the 19th century, with the availability of cheap sugar and flour and chemical raising agents such as bicarbonate of soda (baking soda), cookie factories were able to open up. As the quality of factory-made cookies improved, more people began to buy rather than make their own cookies.

COOKIE-MAKING TODAY

In recent years, consumers have started to turn away from foods containing artificial additives and there has been a resurgence in home-baking. Time-saving kitchen devices have helped to speed up cookie-making, and the widely available range of more unusual ingredients has opened up the possibilities for modern cooks who can now make just about any cookie they want.

With the help of this book, you can learn everything you will ever need to know about cookie-making – from the basic techniques to the perfect cookie to serve with coffee or tea or a glass of milk.

Teatime cookies

Whether you are taking a five-minute break, entertaining friends for afternoon tea or attempting to stem the hunger pangs of ravenous children, this is the chapter to turn to. Tasty treats range from Chocolate Treacle Snaps – perfect for kids – to more sophisticated Cappuccino Swirls.

Peanut butter and jelly cookies

These cookies are a twist on the original American peanut butter cookie and are a real hit with kids and adults alike. Give them a try – you'll love the crunchy nuts and sweet raspberry centres.

MAKES 20–22

227g/8oz jar crunchy peanut butter (with no added sugar)

75g/3oz/6 tbsp unsalted (sweet) butter, at room temperature, diced

90g/3¹/₂oz/¹/₂ cup golden caster (superfine) sugar

50g/2oz/¹/₄ cup light muscovado (brown) sugar

1 large (US extra large) egg, beaten

150g/5oz/1¹/₄ cups self-raising (self-rising) flour

250g/9oz/scant 1 cup seedless raspberry jam

1 Preheat the oven to 180°C/350°F/Gas 4. Line three or four baking sheets with baking parchment. Put the peanut butter and unsalted butter in a large bowl and beat together until well combined and creamy. Add the caster and muscovado sugars and mix. Add the beaten egg and blend well. Sift in the flour and mix to a stiff dough.

2 Roll the dough into walnut-size balls between the palms of your hands. Place the balls on the prepared baking sheets and gently flatten each one with a fork to make a rough-textured cookie with a ridged surface.

3 Bake for 10–12 minutes, or until cooked but not browned. Using a metal spatula, transfer to a wire rack to cool.

4 Spoon jam on to one cookie and top with a second. Continue to sandwich the cookies in this way.

Nutritional information per cookie: Energy 169kcal/709kJ; Protein 3.4g; Carbohydrate 21g, of which sugars 15.3g; Fat 8.5g, of which saturates 3.2g; Cholesterol 18mg; Calcium 35mg; Fibre 0.8g; Sodium 89mg.

Sugar-topped vanilla cookies

Buttery, crumbly vanilla cookies with an irresistible crunchy sugar topping, these are great as a mid-morning snack but also delicious served with luxury vanilla ice cream for a quick dessert.

MAKES ABOUT 24

115g/4oz/1/2 cup unsalted (sweet) butter, at room temperature, diced
50g/2oz/1/4 cup vanilla caster (superfine) sugar
1 egg, beaten
1.5ml/1/4 tsp vanilla extract
200g/7oz/13/4 cups self-raising (self-rising) flour
45ml/3 tbsp cornflour (cornstarch)

FOR THE TOPPING
1 egg white
15ml/1 tbsp vanilla caster (superfine) sugar
75g/3oz sugar cubes, crushed

1 Preheat the oven to 180°C/350°F/Gas 4. Put the butter and sugar in a bowl and beat until the mixture is light and fluffy. Beat in the egg and vanilla extract. Sift together the flour and cornflour over the mixture and mix to a soft but not sticky dough.

2 Roll the mixture out on a lightly floured surface. Using a flower biscuit (cookie) cutter or ring cutter, stamp out cookies and place on a non-stick baking sheet. Re-roll any trimmings and stamp out more cookies until you have used up all the dough.

3 For the topping, put the egg white in a small bowl and whisk until foamy. Whisk in the vanilla sugar. Using a pastry brush, spread generously on each cookie. Sprinkle with the crushed sugar cubes.

4 Bake for about 15 minutes, or until the topping is just beginning to turn golden brown. Remove from the oven and transfer to a wire rack to cool.

Nutritional information per cookie: Energy 96kcal/405kJ; Protein 1.2g; Carbohydrate 14.2g, of which sugars 6.2g; Fat 4.3g, of which saturates 2.6g; Cholesterol 18mg; Calcium 35mg; Fibre 0.3g; Sodium 66mg.

Greek honey crunch creams

With its scent of liquorice and aniseed, Greek honey lends a wonderful flavour to these cookies. If you like your honey less strong, try using orange blossom or lavender honey instead.

MAKES 20

250g/9oz/2¼ cups self-raising (self-rising) flour
10ml/2 tsp bicarbonate of soda (baking soda)
50g/2oz/¼ cup caster (superfine) sugar
115g/4oz/½ cup unsalted (sweet) butter, diced
finely grated rind of 1 large orange
115g/4oz/½ cup Greek honey

25g/1oz/¼ cup pine nuts or chopped walnuts

FOR THE FILLING
50g/2oz/¼ cup unsalted (sweet) butter, at room temperature, diced
115g/4oz/1 cup icing (confectioners') sugar, sifted
15ml/1 tbsp Greek honey

1 Preheat the oven to 200°C/400°F/Gas 6. Line three or four baking sheets with baking parchment. Sift the flour, bicarbonate of soda and caster sugar into a bowl. Add the butter and rub in until the mixture resembles breadcrumbs. Stir in the orange rind.

2 Put the honey in a small pan and heat until just runny but not hot. Pour over the dry mixture and mix to a firm dough.

3 Divide the dough in half and shape one half into 20 small balls about the size of a hazelnut in its shell. Place the balls on the baking sheets, spaced well apart, and flatten. Bake for 6–8 minutes, until golden brown. Leave to cool on the baking sheets, then transfer the cookies to a wire rack to cool completely.

4 Shape the remaining dough into 20 balls and dip one side of each one into the pine nuts or walnuts. Place the cookies, nut sides up, on the baking sheets, gently flatten and bake for 6–8 minutes, until golden brown. Leave to cool and firm up slightly on the baking sheets before carefully transferring the cookies to a wire rack, still nut sides up, to cool completely.

5 To make the filling, put the butter, sugar and honey in a bowl and beat together until light and fluffy. Use the mixture to sandwich the cookies together in pairs using a plain cookie for the base and a nut-coated one for the top.

Nutritional information per cookie: Energy 164kcal/688kJ; Protein 1.5g; Carbohydrate 23.4g, of which sugars 13.9g; Fat 7.8g, of which saturates 4.4g; Cholesterol 18mg; Calcium 24mg; Fibre 0.4g; Sodium 52mg.

Toffee apple and oat crunchies

An unashamedly addictive mixture of chewy oats, soft apple and wonderfully crunchy toffee, this cookie may not be the most stylish in appearance but it is definitely top of the class for flavour.

MAKES ABOUT 16

150g/5oz/10 tbsp unsalted (sweet) butter

175g/6oz/scant 1 cup light muscovado (brown) sugar

90g/3¹/₂oz/¹/₂ cup granulated (white) sugar

1 large (US extra large) egg, beaten

75g/3oz/²/₃ cup plain (all-purpose) flour

2.5ml/¹/₂ tsp bicarbonate of soda (baking soda)

pinch of salt

250g/9oz/2¹/₂ cups rolled oats

50g/2oz/scant ¹/₂ cup sultanas (golden raisins)

50g/2oz dried apple rings, coarsely chopped

50g/2oz chewy toffees, coarsely chopped

1 Preheat the oven to 180°C/ 350°F/Gas 4. Line two or three baking sheets with baking parchment. In a large bowl, beat together the butter and both sugars until creamy. Add the beaten egg and stir well until combined.

2 Sift together the flour, bicarbonate of soda and salt. Add to the butter, sugar and egg mixture and mix in well. Finally add the oats, sultanas, chopped apple rings and toffee pieces and stir gently until everything is just combined.

3 Using a small ice cream scoop or large tablespoon, place heaps of the mixture spaced well apart on the prepared baking sheets. Bake for about 10–12 minutes, or until the cookies are lightly set in the centre and just beginning to brown at the edges.

4 Remove the cookies from the oven and leave to cool on the baking sheets for a few minutes. Using a metal spatula, transfer the cookies to a wire rack to allow them to cool completely.

Nutritional information per cookie: Energy 249kcal/1047kJ; Protein 3.1g; Carbohydrate 38.8g, of which sugars 23.2g; Fat 10.1g, of which saturates 5.3g; Cholesterol 32mg; Calcium 34mg; Fibre 1.3g; Sodium 79mg.

Apple and elderflower stars

These delicious, crumbly apple cookies are topped with a sweet yet very sharp icing. Packaged in a pretty box, they would make a delightfully festive gift for someone special.

MAKES ABOUT 18

115g/4oz/¹/₂ cup unsalted (sweet)
   butter, at room temperature, diced
75g/3oz/scant ¹/₂ cup caster
   (superfine) sugar
2.5ml/¹/₂ tsp mixed (apple pie) spice
1 large (US extra large) egg yolk
25g/1oz dried apple rings, finely chopped
200g/7oz/1³/₄ cups self-raising
   (self-rising) flour
5–10ml/1–2 tsp milk, if necessary

FOR THE TOPPING

200g/7oz/1³/₄ cups icing
   (confectioners') sugar, sifted
60–90ml/4–6 tbsp elderflower cordial
granulated (white) sugar, for sprinkling

1 Preheat the oven to 190°C/375°F/Gas 5. Cream together the butter and sugar until light and fluffy. Beat in the mixed spice and egg yolk. Add the chopped apple and flour and stir together well. The mixture should form a stiff dough but if it is too dry, add some milk.

2 Roll the dough out on a floured surface to 5mm/¹/₄in thick. Draw a five-pointed star on cardboard. Cut out and use as a template for the cookies. Alternatively, use a star biscuit (cookie) cutter.

3 Place the cookies on non-stick baking sheets and bake for about 10–15 minutes, or until just beginning to brown around the edges. Carefully transfer the cookies to a wire rack to cool.

4 For the topping, sift the icing sugar into a bowl and add just enough elderflower cordial to mix to a thick but pourable consistency.

5 When the cookies are cold, trickle the icing over them. Sprinkle with granulated sugar and leave to set.

Nutritional information per cookie: Energy 157kcal/659kJ; Protein 1.4g; Carbohydrate 26.6g, of which sugars 18.1g; Fat 5.7g, of which saturates 3.4g; Cholesterol 25mg; Calcium 27mg; Fibre 0.4g; Sodium 42mg.

Ginger cookies

These are a supreme treat for ginger lovers – richly spiced cookies packed with chunks of succulent preserved stem ginger. Serve small cookies as an after-dinner treat.

MAKES 30 SMALL OR 20 LARGE COOKIES

350g/12oz/3 cups self-raising (self-rising) flour
pinch of salt
200g/7oz/1 cup golden caster (superfine) sugar
15ml/1 tbsp ground ginger
5ml/1 tsp bicarbonate of soda (baking soda)
115g/4oz/1/2 cup unsalted (sweet) butter
90g/31/2oz/generous 1/4 cup golden (light corn) syrup
1 large (US extra large) egg, beaten
150g/5oz preserved stem ginger in syrup, drained and coarsely chopped

1 Preheat the oven to 160°C/325°F/Gas 3. Line three baking sheets with baking parchment. Sift the flour into a large bowl, add the salt, caster sugar, ground ginger and bicarbonate of soda and stir to combine.

2 Dice the butter and put it in a small pan with the syrup. Heat gently, stirring, until the butter has melted. Set aside to cool until just warm.

3 Pour the butter mixture over the dry ingredients, then add the egg and two-thirds of the ginger. Mix well, then use your hands to bring the dough together. Shape the dough into 20 large or 30 small balls, depending on the size you require. Place them, spaced well apart, on the baking sheets.

4 Gently flatten the balls, then press a few pieces of the remaining preserved stem ginger into the top of each of the cookies. Bake for 12–15 minutes, depending on the size of your cookies, until light golden in colour. Leave to cool for 1 minute on the baking sheets to firm up. Using a metal spatula, transfer to a wire rack to cool completely.

Nutritional information per cookie: Energy 114kcal/479kJ; Protein 1.4g; Carbohydrate 20.4g, of which sugars 11.5g; Fat 3.5g, of which saturates 2.1g; Cholesterol 15mg; Calcium 23mg; Fibre 0.4g; Sodium 42mg.

Cappuccino swirls

A melt-in-the-mouth, mocha-flavoured cookie drizzled with white and dark chocolate is just the thing to have with a mid-morning caffè latte, or with afternoon tea with friends.

MAKES 18

10ml/2 tsp instant coffee powder
10ml/2 tsp boiling water
150g/5oz/1¼ cups plain
   (all-purpose) flour
115g/4oz/½ cup cornflour (cornstarch)
15ml/1 tbsp unsweetened cocoa powder
225g/8oz/1 cup unsalted (sweet) butter,
   at room temperature, diced
50g/2oz/¼ cup golden caster
   (superfine) sugar

FOR THE DECORATION

50g/2oz white chocolate
25g/1oz dark (bittersweet) chocolate

1 Preheat the oven to 190°C/375°F/Gas 5. Line two baking sheets with baking parchment. Put the coffee powder in a cup, add the water and stir until dissolved. Set aside to cool. Sift together the flour, cornflour and cocoa.

2 Put the butter and sugar in a bowl and beat until creamy. Add the coffee and the sifted flour and mix well. Spoon into a piping (pastry) bag fitted with a plain nozzle. Pipe 18 spirals, slightly apart, on to the prepared baking sheets.

3 Bake for 10–15 minutes until firm but not browned. Remove from the oven and leave on the baking sheets for 1 minute. Transfer to a wire rack to cool.

4 Melt the white and dark chocolate separately in heatproof bowls set over a pan of hot water. Place the cooled cookies close together on kitchen paper. Using a teaspoon, take some white chocolate and flick over the cookies to create small lines of chocolate drizzle over them. When all the white chocolate has been used, repeat with the dark chocolate. Leave to set, then remove the cookies from the paper.

Nutritional information per cookie: Energy 179kcal/746kJ; Protein 1.3g; Carbohydrate 18.1g, of which sugars 5.7g; Fat 11.8g, of which saturates 7.3g; Cholesterol 27mg; Calcium 19mg; Fibre 0.5g; Sodium 88mg.

Citrus drops

These soft, cake-like treats are deliciously tangy, with a zesty, crumbly base filled with sweet, sticky lemon or orange curd. The crunchy topping of almonds makes the perfect finish.

MAKES ABOUT 20

175g/6oz/3/4 cup unsalted (sweet)
    butter, at room temperature, diced
150g/5oz/3/4 cup caster
    (superfine) sugar
finely grated rind of 1 large lemon
finely grated rind of 1 orange
2 egg yolks

50g/2oz/1/2 cup ground almonds
225g/8oz/2 cups self-raising
    (self-rising) flour
50ml/10 tsp lemon and/or orange curd
milk, for brushing
flaked (sliced) almonds,
    for sprinkling

1 Preheat the oven to 160°C/325°F/Gas 3. Line two baking sheets with baking parchment. Beat the butter and sugar together until light and fluffy, then stir in the citrus rinds.

2 Stir the egg yolks into the mixture, then add the ground almonds and flour and mix well.

3 Divide the mixture into 20 pieces and shape into balls. Place on the baking sheets. Using the handle of a wooden spoon, make a hole in the centre of each cookie. Put 2.5ml/1/2 tsp lemon or orange curd into each hole and pinch the opening to semi-enclose the curd.

4 Brush the tops of each cookie with milk and sprinkle with flaked almonds. Bake for about 20 minutes until pale golden brown. Leave to cool slightly on the baking sheets to firm up, then transfer to a wire rack to cool completely.

Nutritional information per cookie: Energy 157kcal/658kJ; Protein 2.1g; Carbohydrate 16.8g, of which sugars 8.2g; Fat 9.6g, of which saturates 4.9g; Cholesterol 39mg; Calcium 31mg; Fibre 0.6g; Sodium 55mg.

Shape and bake cookies

The mixture for these simple Maryland-style cookies can be made and stored in the refrigerator. It's so easy to cook some each day – and there's nothing like a warm, freshly baked cookie.

MAKES ABOUT 20

115g/4oz/¹/₂ cup unsalted (sweet) butter, at room temperature, diced

115g/4oz/generous ¹/₂ cup granulated (white) sugar

115g/4oz/generous ¹/₂ cup light muscovado (brown) sugar

1 large (US extra large) egg

5ml/1 tsp vanilla extract

200g/7oz/1³/₄ cups self-raising (self-rising) flour

150g/5oz/scant 1 cup chocolate chips

50g/2oz/¹/₂ cup chopped toasted hazelnuts or walnuts

50g/2oz/scant ¹/₂ cup raisins

1 Preheat the oven to 180°C/ 350°F/Gas 4. Line two baking sheets with baking parchment. Put the butter and sugars in a large bowl and beat together until light and fluffy. Add the egg and vanilla and beat again until combined.

2 Add the flour, chocolate chips, hazelnuts and raisins, and mix together until just blended.

3 Place teaspoonfuls of the cookie mixture, spaced well apart, on the prepared baking sheets. Bake the cookies for about 15 minutes until golden brown.

4 Remove from the oven and leave the cookies on the baking sheets for 5 minutes to firm up, then use a metal spatula to transfer the cookies to a wire rack to cool.

Nutritional information per cookie: Energy 187kcal/786kJ; Protein 2.1g; Carbohydrate 26.5g, of which sugars 18.7g; Fat 8.8g, of which saturates 4.5g; Cholesterol 22mg; Calcium 30mg; Fibre 0.7g; Sodium 41mg.

Chocolate treacle snaps

These elegantly thin, treacle-flavoured snap cookies have a delicate hint of spice and a decorative lick of chocolate on top. They are particularly good with a steaming cup of hot coffee.

MAKES ABOUT 35

90g/3¹/₂oz/7 tbsp unsalted (sweet) butter, diced
175ml/6fl oz/³/₄ cup golden (light corn) syrup
50ml/2fl oz/¹/₄ cup black treacle (molasses)
250g/9oz/2¹/₄ cups plain (all-purpose) flour
150g/5oz/³/₄ cup golden caster (superfine) sugar
5ml/1 tsp bicarbonate of soda (baking soda)
1.5ml/¹/₄ tsp mixed (apple pie) spice
100g/3³/₄oz milk chocolate
100g/3³/₄oz white chocolate

1 Preheat the oven to 180°C/ 350°F/Gas 4. Line two or three baking sheets with baking parchment. Put the butter, syrup and treacle in a small pan. Heat gently, stirring constantly, until the butter has melted. Remove from the heat and set aside until required.

2 Sift the flour into a bowl. Add the sugar, bicarbonate of soda and mixed spice, and mix well. Slowly pour in the butter and treacle mixture and stir to combine well.

3 Place teaspoonfuls of the mixture spaced well apart on the baking sheets. Bake for 10–12 minutes until just browning around the edges. Leave to cool for a few minutes on the baking sheets. When firm enough to handle, transfer the cookies to a wire rack to cool completely.

4 Melt the milk chocolate and white chocolate separately in heatproof bowls set over pans of hot water. Swirl a little of each into the centre of each cookie and leave to set.

Nutritional information per cookie: Energy 109kcal/459kJ; Protein 1.2g; Carbohydrate 18.2g, of which sugars 12.8g; Fat 4g, of which saturates 2.4g; Cholesterol 6mg; Calcium 35mg; Fibre 0.2g; Sodium 38mg.

Coconut and lime macaroons

These pretty pistachio nut-topped cookies are crunchy on the outside and soft and gooey in the centre. The zesty lime topping contrasts wonderfully with the sweet coconut.

MAKES 12–14

4 large (US extra large) egg whites
250g/9oz/3 cups sweetened desiccated
    (dry shredded) coconut
150g/5oz/¾ cup granulated
    (white) sugar
10ml/2 tsp vanilla extract
25g/1oz/¼ cup plain (all-purpose) flour

FOR THE TOPPING

115g/4oz/1 cup icing (confectioners')
    sugar, sifted
grated rind of 1 lime
15–20ml/3–4 tsp lime juice
about 15g/½oz/1 tbsp pistachio nuts,
    chopped

1 Preheat the oven to 180°C/350°F/Gas 4. Line two baking sheets with baking parchment. Put the egg whites, desiccated coconut, sugar, vanilla extract and flour in a large, heavy pan. Mix well.

2 Place over a low heat and cook for 6–8 minutes, stirring constantly to ensure it does not stick. When the mixture becomes the consistency of thick porridge (oatmeal), remove from the heat.

3 Place spoonfuls of the mixture in rocky piles on the lined baking sheets. Bake for 12–13 minutes, until golden brown. Remove from the oven and leave to cool completely on the baking sheets.

4 To make the topping, put the icing sugar and lime rind into a bowl and add enough lime juice to give a thick pouring consistency. Place a spoonful of icing on each macaroon and allow it to drip down the sides. Sprinkle over the pistachio nuts and serve.

VARIATION
If you prefer, make coconut and lemon macaroons by substituting grated lemon rind and juice.

Nutritional information per cookie: Energy 198kcal/830kJ; Protein 2.3g; Carbohydrate 22.4g, of which sugars 21g; Fat 11.7g, of which saturates 9.6g; Cholesterol 0mg; Calcium 18mg; Fibre 2.6g; Sodium 29mg.

Fig and date ravioli

These melt-in-the-mouth cushions of sweet pastry are filled with a delicious mixture of figs, dates and walnuts and dusted with icing sugar. They are ideal for serving with coffee.

MAKES ABOUT 20

375g/13oz packet sweet
    shortcrust pastry
milk, for brushing
icing (confectioners') sugar, sifted,
    for dusting

FOR THE FILLING
115g/4oz/²/₃ cup ready-to-eat dried figs
50g/2oz/¹/₃ cup stoned (pitted) dates
15g/¹/₂oz/1 tbsp chopped walnuts
10ml/2 tsp lemon juice
15ml/1 tbsp clear honey

1 Preheat the oven to 180°C/ 350°F/Gas 4. To make the filling, put the figs, dates, chopped walnuts, lemon juice and honey into a food processor and blend to a paste.

2 Roll out half of the pastry on a floured surface to a square. Place spoonfuls of the fig paste on the pastry in rows at equal intervals. Roll out the remaining pastry to a slightly larger square. Dampen around each spoonful of filling.

3 Place the second sheet of pastry on top and press together around each mound of filling. Using a pastry wheel, cut squares between the mounds of filling. Place on non-stick baking sheets and brush the tops with a little milk. Bake for about 15–20 minutes until golden.

4 Using a metal spatula, transfer the cookies to a wire rack to cool. When cool, dust with icing sugar.

Nutritional information per cookie: Energy 111kcal/464kJ; Protein 1.5g; Carbohydrate 13.9g, of which sugars 5.3g; Fat 5.9g, of which saturates 1.7g; Cholesterol 3mg; Calcium 31mg; Fibre 0.9g; Sodium 79mg.

Butter cookies

These crunchy, buttery cookies make a tasty afternoon treat served with a cup of tea or a glass of milk. The dough can be made in advance and chilled until you are ready to bake them.

MAKES 25–30

175g/6oz/³⁄₄ cup unsalted (sweet) butter, at room temperature, diced
90g/3¹⁄₂oz/¹⁄₂ cup golden caster (superfine) sugar
250g/9oz/2¹⁄₄ cups plain (all-purpose) flour
demerara (raw) sugar, for coating

1 Put the butter and sugar together in a large bowl and beat until light and fluffy. Add the flour and, using your hands, gradually work it in until the mixture forms a smooth dough. Roll into a sausage shape 30cm/ 12in long, then pat the sides flat to form either a square or triangular log.

2 Sprinkle a thick layer of demerara sugar on a piece of baking parchment. Press each side of the dough into the sugar to coat.

3 Wrap in clear film (plastic wrap) and chill in the refrigerator for about 30 minutes until firm. Meanwhile, preheat the oven to 160°C/325°F/Gas 3.

4 When ready to bake, remove the dough from the refrigerator and unwrap. Cut into thick slices and place slightly apart on non-stick baking sheets. Bake for 20 minutes until just beginning to turn brown. Remove from the oven and transfer the cookies to a wire rack to cool.

Nutritional information per cookie: Energy 84kcal/350kJ; Protein 0.8g; Carbohydrate 9.6g, of which sugars 3.3g; Fat 4.9g, of which saturates 3.1g; Cholesterol 12mg; Calcium 14mg; Fibre 0.3g; Sodium 36mg.

Cookies for kids

There's nothing quite like coming home from school to a plate of freshly baked cookies and a glass of milk. This chapter is packed with fabulous, fun ideas that kids will love, from simple cookies with pretty sugar icing to adorable Puppy Faces and indulgent Ice Cream Sandwiches which are sure to be a hit at birthday parties.

Butter gems

These tiny shortbread-based cookies are topped with rosettes of soft buttercream and a pretty sprinkling of brightly coloured sugar. They make a great treat for even the smallest of mouths.

MAKES ABOUT 40

115g/4oz/¹/₂ cup unsalted (sweet)
   butter, at room temperature, diced
50g/2oz/¹/₄ cup caster (superfine) sugar
175g/6oz/1¹/₂ cups plain
   (all-purpose) flour

FOR THE DECORATION

50g/2oz/4 tbsp unsalted (sweet) butter,
   at room temperature, diced
5ml/1 tsp vanilla extract
90g/3¹/₂oz/³/₄ cup icing
   (confectioners') sugar
25g/1oz/2 tbsp granulated (white) sugar
green, lilac or pink food colourings

1 Put the butter and the sugar in a bowl and beat until smooth and creamy. Add the flour and mix to form a thick paste. Turn the dough on to a floured surface and knead until smooth. Wrap and chill for at least 30 minutes.

2 Preheat the oven to 180°C/350°F/Gas 4. Grease two baking sheets. Roll out the dough on a lightly floured surface and cut out rounds using a 3.5cm/1¹/₄in cookie cutter. Space apart on the baking sheets and bake for 10 minutes until pale golden. Transfer to a wire rack to cool completely.

3 To decorate, beat the butter with the vanilla extract and icing sugar until smooth and creamy. Spoon the buttercream into a piping (pastry) bag fitted with a star-shaped nozzle, then pipe a rosette on to each cookie.

4 Put the granulated sugar into a small bowl and mix in several drops of the food colouring. Sprinkle a little of the coloured sugar over the cookies.

Nutritional information per cookie: Energy 57kcal/238kJ; Protein 0.5g; Carbohydrate 6.4g, of which sugars 3.1g; Fat 3.4g, of which saturates 2.2g; Cholesterol 9mg; Calcium 8mg; Fibre 0.1g; Sodium 25mg.

Flower power cookies

Look out for little piped sugar flower decorations in the supermarket. Try to buy some that are brightly coloured as they contrast better with the pretty pastel-coloured icing.

MAKES 28

225g/8oz/2 cups plain (all-purpose) flour
175g/6oz/³/₄ cup unsalted (sweet) butter, chilled and diced
finely grated rind of 1 orange
130g/4¹/₄ oz/²/₃ cup light muscovado (brown) sugar
1 egg yolk

FOR THE DECORATION

30ml/2 tbsp orange juice
200g/7oz/1³/₄ cups icing (confectioners') sugar
green, yellow and orange food colourings
multi-coloured sugared flowers

1 Put the flour, butter and orange rind into a food processor and process until mixture resembles breadcrumbs. Add the sugar and egg yolk and process until mixture starts to bind together. Turn out on to a floured surface and knead into a dough. Shape into a ball, wrap and chill for 30 minutes.

2 Preheat the oven to 180°C/350°F/Gas 4. Grease two baking sheets. Roll out the dough thinly and cut out rounds using a fluted cookie cutter 6cm/2¹/₂in in diameter. Transfer to the baking sheets, spacing them apart. Bake for 12–15 minutes until golden, then transfer to a wire rack to cool.

3 Put the orange juice in a bowl and stir in the icing sugar until the mixture has the consistency of thick pouring cream. Divide the mixture among three bowls and stir a few drops of different food colouring into each bowl. Spoon some green icing on to one third of the cookies. Top with a flower. Decorate the remaining cookies with the other colours. Leave to set for about 1 hour.

Nutritional information per cookie: 123kcal/516kJ; Protein 1g; Carbohydrate 18.7g, of which sugars 12.5g; Fat 5.4g, of which saturates 3.3g; Cholesterol 21mg; Calcium 20mg; Fibre 0.3g; Sodium 39mg.

Pink sugared hearts

Pretty and pink, these delightful little heart-shaped cookies are always a big hit with Barbie-loving girls and are great at birthday parties. Rolling the edges of the cookies in coloured sugar to accentuate their shape really adds to the fun of decorating.

MAKES 32

225g/8oz/2 cups plain
(all-purpose) flour
175g/6oz/3/4 cup unsalted (sweet)
butter, chilled and diced
130g/41/4oz/2/3 cup caster
(superfine) sugar
1 egg yolk

FOR THE DECORATION
50g/2oz/1/4 cup granulated (white) sugar
pink food colouring
225g/8oz/2 cups icing
(confectioners') sugar
30–45ml/2–3 tbsp lemon juice

1 Preheat the oven to 180°C/350°F/Gas 4. Grease two baking sheets.

2 Put the flour and diced butter into a food processor, then process until the mixture resembles fine breadcrumbs. Add the sugar and egg yolk to the food processor and process until the mixture begins to form a ball.

3 Turn the dough out on to a lightly floured surface and knead until smooth. Shape the dough into a ball, wrap in clear film (plastic wrap) and chill for at least 30 minutes.

4 Working in batches, roll out the dough thinly on a floured surface and cut out heart shapes using a 5cm/2in cutter. Transfer to the baking sheets, spacing them apart. Bake for 10 minutes, or until pale golden. Transfer to a wire rack to cool.

5 To decorate, put the granulated sugar in a bowl and add a small dot of pink food colouring. Using the back of a teaspoon, work the food colouring into the sugar until it is completely pink.

6 Put the icing sugar in a separate bowl and add 30ml/2 tbsp of the lemon juice, stirring until smooth but spreadable. If the paste is too thick stir in a little more lemon juice. Using a metal spatula spread a little icing on to each cookie, to within 5mm/1/4in of the edge. Turn each iced cookie on its side and gently roll in the coloured sugar so that the edges of the icing become coated in pink sugar. Leave the cookies to set for about 1 hour.

Nutritional information per cookie: Energy 265kcal/1126kJ; Protein 1g; Carbohydrate 58.2g, of which sugars 52.9g; Fat 4.8g, of which saturates 2.9g; Cholesterol 18mg; Calcium 38mg; Fibre 0.2g; Sodium 37mg.

Jammie bodgers

These buttery cookies are an absolute classic. Sandwiched with buttercream and a generous dollop of strawberry jam, they make a perfect snack served with a glass of milk at teatime, or are equally good wrapped tightly, and popped in a lunchbox as a post-sandwich treat.

MAKES 20

225g/8oz/2 cups plain (all-purpose) flour
175g/6oz/¾ cup unsalted (sweet) butter, chilled and diced
130g/4¼oz/ ⅔ cup caster (superfine) sugar
1 egg yolk

FOR THE FILLING

50g/2oz/¼ cup unsalted (sweet) butter, at room temperature, diced
90g/3½oz/¾ cup icing (confectioners') sugar
60–75ml/4 –5 tbsp strawberry jam

1 Put the flour and butter in a food processor and process until the mixture resembles breadcrumbs. Add the sugar and egg yolk and process until the mixture starts to form a dough. Knead on a floured surface until smooth. Shape into a ball, wrap and chill for at least 30 minutes.

2 Preheat the oven to 180°C/350°F/Gas 4. Grease two baking sheets. Roll out the dough thinly and cut out rounds using a 6cm/2½in cookie cutter. You need 40 rounds.

3 Place half the rounds on a baking sheet. Using a heart-shaped cutter, 2cm/¾in in diameter, cut out the centres of the remaining rounds. Place these on another baking sheet.

4 Bake for 12 minutes until pale golden. Transfer to a wire rack and leave until cold. Beat the butter and sugar until smooth and creamy. Spread a little buttercream on to each whole cookie. Spoon a little jam on to the buttercream, then press the cut-out cookies on top.

Nutritional information per cookie: Energy 166kcal/695kJ; Protein 1.2g; Carbohydrate 22.4g, of which sugars 13.8g; Fat 8.6g, of which saturates 5.4g; Cholesterol 22mg; Calcium 24mg; Fibre 0.4g; Sodium 65mg.

Peanut crunch cookies

These delicious sweet and nutty cookies are so easy to make. They puff up into lovely domed rounds during baking, giving them a really professional look. If you prefer cookies with a slightly less nutty texture, use smooth peanut butter rather than the crunchy variety.

MAKES 25

115g/4oz/¹/₂ cup unsalted (sweet) butter, at room temperature, diced
115g/4oz/generous ¹/₂ cup light muscovado (brown) sugar
1 egg
150g/5oz/1¹/₄ cups self-raising (self-rising) flour
2.5ml/¹/₂ tsp baking powder
150g/5oz/generous ¹/₂ cup crunchy peanut butter
icing (confectioners') sugar, for dusting

1 Preheat the oven to 190°C/375°F/Gas 5. Lightly grease two large baking sheets.

2 Put the butter and sugar in a bowl and beat until pale and creamy. Beat in the egg, then add the flour, baking powder and peanut butter. Beat until mixed.

3 Place heaped teaspoonfuls of the mixture on to the baking sheets; spaced well apart.

4 Bake the cookies for about 20 minutes until risen; they will still be quite soft to the touch.

5 Take the cookies out of the oven and leave them to cool slightly on the baking sheets for about 5 minutes, then carefully transfer the cookies from the sheets to a wire rack to cool completely.

6 To serve, lightly dust the cookies with a little icing sugar.

Nutritional information per cookie: Energy 112kcal/466kJ; Protein 2.1g; Carbohydrate 10.3g, of which sugars 5.3g; Fat 7.2g, of which saturates 3.2g; Cholesterol 18mg; Calcium 15mg; Fibre 0.5g; Sodium 50mg.

Stained-glass windows

Baking coloured sweets inside a cookie frame creates a stunning stained-glass effect, particularly if you hang the cookies in a place where the light can shine through. The centre will stay brittle for just a day or so before softening, so don't be tempted to hang them up for too long.

MAKES 12–14

175g/6oz/1¹/2 cups plain
(all-purpose) flour
2.5ml/¹/2 tsp bicarbonate of soda
(baking soda)
2.5ml/¹/2 tsp ground cinnamon
75g/3oz/6 tbsp unsalted (sweet)
butter, chilled and diced

75g/3oz/scant ¹/2 cup caster
(superfine) sugar
30ml/2 tbsp golden (light
corn) syrup
1 egg yolk
150g/5oz brightly coloured, clear
boiled sweets (hard candies)

1 Put the flour, bicarbonate of soda, cinnamon and butter into a food processor. Process until the mixture resembles breadcrumbs. Add the sugar, syrup and egg yolk and process until the mixture starts to form a dough. Turn the dough out on to a lightly floured surface and knead until smooth. Wrap and chill in the refrigerator for at least 30 minutes.

2 Preheat the oven to 180°C/350°F/Gas 4. Line two large baking sheets with baking parchment. Roll out the dough thinly on a lightly floured surface. Cut into 6cm/2¹/2in wide strips, then cut diagonally across the strips to create about 12 diamond shapes. Transfer the diamond shapes to the baking sheets, spacing them apart. Cut out a smaller diamond shape from the centre of each cookie and remove to leave a 1cm/¹/2in frame. Using a skewer, make a hole at one end of each cookie (large enough to thread fine ribbon). Bake for 5 minutes.

3 Meanwhile, lightly crush the sweets (still in their wrappers) by tapping them gently with the end of a rolling pin. Remove the cookies from the oven and quickly fill the centre of each one with two crushed sweets of the same colour.

4 Bake for a further 5 minutes until the sweets have melted. Use a skewer to re-mark the skewer holes if they have shrunk. If the sweets haven't spread to fill the centre, carefully spread the melted sweets with the tip of a skewer.

5 Leave the cookies on the baking parchment until the centres are hard, then peel away the paper. Thread fine ribbon of different lengths through the holes in the cookies, then hang as decorations.

Nutritional information per cookie: Energy 145kcal/612kJ; Protein 1.2g; Carbohydrate 26.4g, of which sugars 16.8g; Fat 4.6g, of which saturates 2.8g; Cholesterol 11mg; Calcium 22mg; Fibre 0.4g; Sodium 42mg.

Jelly bean cones

Chocolate-dipped cookie cones filled with jelly beans make great treats for kids of all ages. The filled cones look very pretty arranged in narrow glasses or other small containers to keep them upright. This way they can double as a tasty treat and a delightful table decoration.

MAKES 10

3 egg whites
**90g/3¹/₂oz/¹/₂ cup caster
   (superfine) sugar**
**25g/1oz/2 tbsp unsalted (sweet)
   butter, melted**
**40g/1¹/₂oz/¹/₃ cup plain
   (all-purpose) flour**
30ml/2 tbsp single (light) cream
90g/3¹/₂oz plain (semisweet) chocolate
**jelly beans or other small sweets
   (candies)**

1 Preheat the oven to 190°C/375°F/ Gas 5. Line two baking sheets with baking parchment and grease. Put the egg whites and sugar in a bowl and whisk lightly with a fork until the egg whites are broken up. Add the melted butter, flour and cream and stir well to make a smooth batter.

2 Place a rounded tablespoon of the mixture on one side of a baking sheet. Spread to a 9cm/3¹/₂in round with the back of the spoon. Spoon more mixture on to the other side of the baking sheet and spread out to make another round. Bake for 8–10 minutes until the edges are deep golden. Spoon two more rounds of mixture on to the second baking sheet.

3 Remove the first batch from the oven and replace with the second batch. Peel away the paper from the cookies and roll them into cones. Leave to set. Continue until you have made 10 cones. Melt the chocolate in a heatproof bowl set over a pan of simmering water. Dip the wide ends of the cookies in the chocolate and prop them inside small glasses to set. Fill with jelly beans.

Nutritional information per cookie: Energy 160kcal/670kJ; Protein 1.9g; Carbohydrate 18.3g, of which sugars 15.2g; Fat 9.3g, of which saturates 5.8g; Cholesterol 18mg; Calcium 18mg; Fibre 0.4g; Sodium 66mg.

Secret message cookies

What these cookies lack in substance, they certainly make up for in their fun capacity. A simpler variation on the traditional Chinese fortune cookie, these are great for older kids who can prepare birthday messages, jokes or predictions to tuck into the cookies as soon as they're baked.

MAKES 18

3 egg whites
50g/2oz/1/2 cup icing
    (confectioners') sugar
40g/11/2oz/3 tbsp unsalted (sweet)
    butter, melted
50g/2oz/1/2 cup plain (all-purpose) flour

1 Preheat the oven to 200°C/400°F/Gas 6. Line two baking sheets with baking parchment and grease. Cut a piece of paper into 18 small strips, measuring 6 x 2cm/21/2 x 3/4in. Write a message on each one.

2 Lightly whisk the egg whites and icing sugar until the whites are broken up. Add the melted butter and flour and beat until smooth. Using a 10ml/2 tsp measure, spoon a little of the paste on to one baking sheet and spread to a 7.5cm/3in round with the back of a spoon. Add two more spoonfuls of mixture to the baking sheet and shape in the same way. Bake for 6 minutes until golden. Prepare three more cookies on the second baking sheet.

3 Remove the first batch of cookies from the oven and replace with the second batch. Working quickly, peel a hot cookie from the paper and fold it in half, tucking a message inside the fold. Rest the cookie over the rim of a glass and, gently, fold again. Fold the remaining two cookies in the same way. Continue to bake and shape the remaining cookies in the same way until all the batter and messages have been used.

Nutritional information per cookie: Energy 38kcal/160kJ; Protein 0.6g; Carbohydrate 5.1g, of which sugars 3g; Fat 1.9g, of which saturates 1.2g; Cholesterol 5mg; Calcium 6mg; Fibre 0.1g; Sodium 19mg.

Tree cookies

These cookies look really effective with their chocolate cookie "trunks" and brightly coloured "fruits". Kids will love helping to decorate them. Arrange the cookies in a line on the tea table.

MAKES 10

50g/2oz/¼ cup unsalted (sweet) butter,
   at room temperature, diced
115g/4oz/½ cup light muscovado
   (brown) sugar
1 egg
150g/5oz/1¼ cups self-raising
   (self-rising) flour
2.5ml/½ tsp bicarbonate of soda
   (baking soda)
finely grated rind of 1 lemon

FOR THE DECORATION

50g/2oz/½ cup icing
   (confectioners') sugar
10ml/2 tsp lemon juice
10 milk chocolate fingers
brightly coloured sweets (candies),
   such as m&ms

1 Preheat the oven to 180°C/ 350°F/Gas 4. Grease two large baking sheets.

2 Beat the butter and sugar together in a bowl until smooth and creamy. Beat in the egg. Add the flour, bicarbonate of soda and lemon rind and mix until smooth.

3 Place five large spoonfuls of the mixture on to each baking sheet, spacing them well apart. Bake for about 15 minutes until the cookies have risen.

4 Leave the cookies on the baking sheet for 5 minutes to firm up, then transfer to a wire rack to cool.

5 To decorate the cookies, mix together the icing sugar and lemon juice to make a thick paste. Use a little paste to secure one end of a chocolate finger to each cookie.

6 Attach the coloured sweets in the same way, securing each one with a little paste. Leave the cookies to set for at least 1 hour. (Handle the decorated cookies with care.)

Nutritional information per cookie: Energy 162kcal/681kJ; Protein 1.3g; Carbohydrate 24g, of which sugars 21.6g; Fat 7.2g, of which saturates 2.8g; Cholesterol 30mg; Calcium 24mg; Fibre 0.2g; Sodium 54mg.

Party bracelets

Make these tiny cookies a day or two in advance and simply thread on to fine ribbon together with an assortment of brightly coloured sweets on the day of the party.

MAKES 22

50g/2oz/¹⁄₄ cup unsalted (sweet) butter, at room temperature, diced
115g/4oz/generous ¹⁄₂ cup caster (superfine) sugar
5ml/1 tsp vanilla extract
pink or green food colouring
1 egg
200g/7oz/1³⁄₄ cups self-raising (self-rising) flour

FOR THE DECORATION

2 large bags of boiled sweets (hard candies) with holes in the centre
narrow pastel-coloured ribbon, for threading

1 Preheat the oven to 180°C/350°F/Gas 4. Grease two baking sheets. Beat the butter, sugar and vanilla extract together until pale and creamy. Add a dash of food colouring, then beat in the egg. Add the flour and mix to form a dough.

2 Turn the dough on to a floured surface and roll out under the palms of your hands into two long, thin sausage shapes, each about 40cm/16in long. Cut each roll across into 5mm/¹⁄₄in lengths.

3 Space the cookies apart on the baking sheets and chill for about 30 minutes.

4 Bake for 8 minutes until slightly risen and beginning to colour. Using a skewer, make holes for the ribbon to be threaded through. Transfer to a wire rack to cool.

5 Thread the cookies on to 20cm/8in lengths of ribbon, alternating with the sweets. Tie the ends of the ribbons together to finish.

Nutritional information per cookie: Energy 72kcal/303kJ; Protein 1.2g; Carbohydrate 12.5g, of which sugars 5.6g; Fat 2.2g, of which saturates 1.3g; Cholesterol 13mg; Calcium 17mg; Fibre 0.3g; Sodium 18mg.

Train cookies

These simple party biscuits are so easy yet incredibly effective, particularly if you let them trail across the party table. The quantity makes enough for two trains, but double it if required.

MAKES 10

150g/5oz/1¼ cups plain
   (all-purpose) flour
90g/3½oz/7 tbsp unsalted (sweet)
   butter, chilled, diced
50g/2oz/½ cup golden icing
   (confectioners') sugar
1 egg yolk
5ml/1 tsp vanilla extract

FOR THE DECORATION

40g/1½oz/3 tbsp butter, softened
75g/3oz/⅔ cup golden icing
   (confectioners') sugar
blue food colouring
large bag of liquorice allsorts

1 Put the flour and butter in a food processor. Process until the mixture resembles fine breadcrumbs. Add the sugar, egg yolk and vanilla; blend to a smooth dough. Wrap and chill for 30 minutes.

2 Preheat the oven to 200°C/400°F/Gas 6. Grease a large baking sheet. Roll out the dough and cut 7.5 x 4cm/3 x 1½in rectangles. Cut two 3 x 2cm/1¼ x ¾in rectangles and secure to the top of the larger rectangles for the engines. Place on the baking sheet and bake for 10 minutes until pale golden. Leave for 2 minutes, then transfer to a wire rack to cool completely.

3 Put the butter and icing sugar in a bowl with a drop of food colouring and beat until smooth. Chop plenty of the liquorice into small dice. Spread a little buttercream along one long side of the biscuits except the engines and press the chopped sweets into the buttercream. Halve some square sweets and secure to the engines and another piece on the front of the engine for the funnel. Secure two wheels on all biscuits. Arrange in a trail across the table.

Nutritional information per cookie: Energy 174kcal/728kJ; Protein 1.8g; Carbohydrate 24.8g, of which sugars 13.3g; Fat 8.1g, of which saturates 4.9g; Cholesterol 39mg; Calcium 32mg; Fibre 0.5g; Sodium 57mg.

Gold medals

These cookies are great for kids' parties. You can present each child with a huge cookie medal when they sit down at the table, or hand them out to winners of party games.

MAKES 10

50g/2oz/¼ cup unsalted (sweet) butter, at room temperature, diced
115g/4oz/generous ½ cup caster (superfine) sugar
1 egg
150g/5oz/1¼ cups self-raising (self-rising) flour
1.5ml/¼ tsp bicarbonate of soda (baking soda)

FOR THE DECORATION
1 egg white
200g/7oz/1¾ cups icing (confectioners') sugar
small brightly coloured sweets (candies)

1 Preheat the oven to 180°C/350°F/Gas 4. Grease two baking sheets with a little butter. Beat together the butter and sugar until smooth and creamy, then beat in the egg. Add the flour and bicarbonate of soda and mix well.

2 Place large spoonfuls of the mixture on the baking sheets, spacing them well apart. Bake for about 15 minutes, or until pale golden and slightly risen. Using a skewer, make quite a large hole in the cookie, 1cm/½in from the edge. Transfer to a wire rack and leave to cool.

3 To make the icing, beat the egg white in a bowl using a wooden spoon. Gradually beat in the icing sugar to make a thick paste that just holds its shape. Spoon the icing into a small plastic bag and snip off the merest tip.

4 Write icing messages in the centre of the cookies. Secure a circle of sweets around the edge of each cookie with a little of the icing, then leave to set. Carefully thread each cookie with a piece of ribbon.

Nutritional information per cookie: Energy 221kcal/936kJ; Protein 2.5g; Carbohydrate 44.6g, of which sugars 33.2g; Fat 4.9g, of which saturates 2.8g; Cholesterol 30mg; Calcium 42mg; Fibre 0.5g; Sodium 46mg.

Name cookies

You could decorate these cookies for children coming to a party, either in vibrant, bright colours or in more delicate pastels. It can be a fun idea to prop a name cookie up against the glass at each place setting around the tea table and let the children find their own seats.

MAKES 20

200g/7oz/scant 1 cup unsalted (sweet)
  butter, chilled and diced
300g/11oz/2³/₄ cups plain
  (all-purpose) flour
finely grated rind of 1 orange
90g/3¹/₂oz/³/₄ cup icing (confectioners')
  sugar
2 egg yolks

FOR THE DECORATION

1 egg white
200g/7oz/1³/₄ cups icing sugar
2 different food colourings
silver balls or jelly beans

1 Put the butter, flour and orange rind in a food processor and process until the mixture resembles fine breadcrumbs. Add the icing sugar and egg yolks and blend until smooth. Wrap the dough in clear film (plastic wrap) and chill for 30 minutes.

2 Preheat the oven to 200°C/400°F/Gas 6. Grease two baking sheets. Roll out the dough on a floured surface and cut out cookies in a variety of shapes, such as squares, hearts and rounds. Make sure each cookie is at least 7.5cm/3in across.

3 Transfer the cookies to the baking sheets, spacing them apart, and bake for 10–12 minutes until pale golden around the edges. Leave on the baking sheet for 2 minutes to firm up, then transfer to a wire rack to cool completely.

4 For the icing, beat the egg white and icing sugar together until smooth. Divide between two bowls, then beat a few drops of food colouring into each to make two different colours. Spoon the different icings into separate plastic bags and squeeze into one corner. Cut off the tip from each bag so the icing can be piped in a thin line, then write the names of guests on the cookies. Pipe decorative borders around the edges of the cookies.

5 Chop the jelly beans, if using, into small pieces. Secure the silver balls or jelly beans on to the icing on the cookies to finish. Leave the cookies to set for at least 1 hour.

Nutritional information per cookie: Energy 189kcal/795kJ; Protein 2g; Carbohydrate 26.9g, of which sugars 15.4g; Fat 9g, of which saturates 5.4g; Cholesterol 41mg; Calcium 33mg; Fibre 0.5g; Sodium 66mg.

Orange biscotti

These crisp, crunchy cookies are based on a traditional Italian recipe in which the cookies are packed with nuts and twice baked. This version is flavoured with orange instead of the nuts and shaped into long, thin sticks. They are a little softer than the classic biscotti, which are very hard.

MAKES ABOUT 20

50g/2oz/¹⁄₄ cup unsalted (sweet) butter, at room temperature, diced
90g/3¹⁄₂oz/¹⁄₂ cup light muscovado (brown) sugar
1 egg
finely grated rind of 1 small orange, plus 10ml/2 tsp juice
175g/6oz/1¹⁄₂ cups self-raising (self-rising) flour
7.5ml/1¹⁄₂ tsp baking powder
good pinch of ground cinnamon
50g/2oz/¹⁄₂ cup polenta
icing (confectioners') sugar, for dusting

1 Preheat the oven to 160°C/ 325°F/Gas 3. Grease a baking sheet. Beat together the butter and sugar until smooth. Beat in the egg, then the orange rind, juice, flour, baking powder, cinnamon and polenta.

2 Tip the mixture on to a lightly floured surface and knead. Place the dough on the baking sheet and flatten with the palm of your hand to make a rectangle about 25 x 18cm/10 x 7in.

3 Bake for 25 minutes, then remove from the oven and leave to stand for 5 minutes until slightly cooled. Using a sharp knife, carefully cut the mixture widthways into thin sticks, about 1cm/¹⁄₂in wide.

4 Space the cookies out slightly on the baking sheet, then bake for a further 20 minutes until crisp. Transfer the biscotti to a wire rack and leave to cool. Serve dusted with a little icing sugar.

Nutritional information per cookie: Energy 80kcal/337kJ; Protein 1.4g; Carbohydrate 13.6g, of which sugars 5.1g; Fat 2.5g, of which saturates 1.4g; Cholesterol 15mg; Calcium 17mg; Fibre 0.3g; Sodium 19mg.

Ice cream sandwiches

Home-made wafer cookies have a flavour unlike anything you can buy at the supermarket. These crisp, nutty cookies make perfect ice cream sandwiches for a summer-time treat. They're also fun to make and are a good accompaniment to almost any fruity or creamy dessert.

MAKES 6 SANDWICHES

50g/2oz/¹/₄ cup unsalted (sweet) butter
2 egg whites
75g/3oz/scant ¹/₂ cup caster
  (superfine) sugar
50g/2oz/¹/₂ cup plain (all-purpose) flour
40g/1¹/₂oz/scant ¹/₂ cup ground
  almonds
30ml/2 tbsp flaked (sliced)
  almonds (optional)
raspberry ripple or vanilla ice cream,
  to serve
icing (confectioners') sugar, for dusting

1 Preheat the oven to 200°C/ 400°F/Gas 6. Line two large baking sheets with baking parchment.

2 Put the butter in a small pan and melt over a very low heat. Remove from the heat.

3 Put the egg whites and sugar in a bowl and whisk lightly with a fork until the egg whites are broken up. Add the flour, melted butter and ground almonds and mix until the mixture is evenly combined.

4 Drop 6 level tablespoonfuls of mixture on to each baking sheet, spacing them well apart. Spread the mixture to circles about 7cm/2³/₄in in diameter. Sprinkle with almonds, if using, and bake for 10–12 minutes until golden around the edges. Peel away the paper and transfer to a wire rack to cool.

5 Place a scoop of slightly softened ice cream on to one cookie and top with another, gently pressing them together. Dust with sugar and serve.

Nutritional information per cookie: Energy 184kcal/771kJ; Protein 3.3g; Carbohydrate 20.1g, of which sugars 13.5g; Fat 10.7g, of which saturates 4.7g; Cholesterol 18mg; Calcium 36mg; Fibre 0.8g; Sodium 73mg.

Silly faces

These funny little characters can be made using almost any type of cookie mix, as long as the baked cookies are quite big and not too craggy. Silly faces are great fun for kids to decorate.

MAKES 14

115g/4oz/¹/2 cup unsalted (sweet) butter, at room temperature, diced
115g/4oz/generous ¹/2 cup golden caster (superfine) sugar
1 egg
115g/4oz/scant ¹/3 cup golden (light corn) syrup
400g/14oz/3¹/2 cups self-raising (self-rising) flour

FOR THE DECORATION

75g/3oz/6 tbsp unsalted (sweet) butter, at room temperature, diced
150g/5oz/1¹/4 cups icing (confectioners') sugar
strawberry, apple or liquorice strands
glacé (candied) cherries, halved
red and black writer icing tubes
small multi-coloured sweets (candies)

1 Put the butter and sugar in a bowl and beat until pale and creamy. Beat in the egg and golden syrup, add the flour and mix to a paste. Turn on to a floured surface and knead until smooth. Wrap in clear film (plastic wrap) and chill for 30 minutes.

2 Preheat the oven to 180°C/350°F/Gas 4. Grease two baking sheets. Roll out the chilled dough on a floured surface and cut out rounds using a 9cm/3¹/2in cookie cutter. Transfer to the baking sheets, re-rolling the trimmings to make more cookies. Bake for 10–12 minutes until turning golden around the edges. Transfer to a wire rack to cool.

3 To decorate, beat together the butter and icing sugar until smooth. Spread a little buttercream along the top edge of each cookie, then secure the strawberry, apple or liquorice strands to make hair.

4 Use a dot of buttercream to secure a cherry to the middle of each cookie for a nose. Pipe eyes and mouths using the writer icing tubes, then add halved sweets, attached with buttercream, for the centres of the eyes.

Nutritional information per cookie: Energy 300kcal/1261kJ; Protein 3.2g; Carbohydrate 48g, of which sugars 26.7g; Fat 11.9g, of which saturates 7.2g; Cholesterol 43mg; Calcium 116mg; Fibre 0.9g; Sodium 213mg.

Puppy faces

These cookies are decorated with the widely available, white "ready-to-roll" icing, but you can knead in a little black, brown or yellow food colouring to make different coloured dogs.

MAKES 10

100g/3³/₄oz/scant 1 cup plain
  (all-purpose) flour
50g/2oz/¹/₂ cup rolled oats
2.5ml/¹/₂ tsp mixed (apple pie) spice
50g/2oz/¹/₄ cup unsalted (sweet) butter,
  chilled and diced
100g/3³/₄oz/generous ¹/₂ cup caster
  (superfine) sugar
1 egg yolk

FOR THE DECORATION
60ml/4 tbsp apricot jam
250g/9oz white ready-to-roll icing
10 round coloured sweets (candies)
black and red writer icing tubes
icing (confectioners') sugar, for dusting

1 Put the flour, rolled oats, spice and butter into the food processor. Process until the mixture resembles fine breadcrumbs. Add the sugar, egg yolk and 5ml/1 tsp water and blend until the mixture forms a ball. Turn the dough on to a floured surface and knead until smooth. Wrap in clear film (plastic wrap) and chill for 30 minutes.

2 Preheat oven to 200°C/400°F/Gas 6. Grease a baking sheet. Roll out dough on a floured surface and cut out rounds with a 6cm/2¹/₂in cutter. Transfer to the baking sheet. Bake for 12 minutes. Allow to cool on a wire rack.

3 Press the jam through a sieve (strainer). Brush over each cookie to within 5mm/¹/₄in of the edge. Roll out half the icing thinly on a surface dusted with icing sugar. Cut out ten rounds using the cutter and lay one over each cookie.

4 For eyes, halve the coloured sweets, brush the icing with water and press the sweets into the cookies. Pipe noses, mouths and tongues using the writer tubes. For ears, divide the remaining icing into 20 pieces. Roll each piece into a ball and flatten to make a pear shape. Lightly brush the icing with water and secure ears.

Nutritional information per cookie: Energy 251kcal/1063kJ; Protein 2.1g; Carbohydrate 52.2g, of which sugars 40.9g; Fat 5.2g, of which saturates 2.8g; Cholesterol 31mg; Calcium 37mg; Fibre 0.7g; Sodium 38mg.

Gingerbread house cookies

For a party of young children, these gingerbread house cookies provide plenty of entertainment. You could incorporate a house-decorating session as one of the party games, allowing the children to design their own house and take it home after the party.

MAKES 10

115g/4oz/1/2 cup unsalted (sweet)
   butter, at room temperature, diced
115g/4oz/generous 1/2 cup light
   muscovado (brown) sugar
1 egg
115g/4oz/scant 1/3 cup black treacle
   (molasses) or golden (light corn) syrup
400g/14oz/31/2 cups self-raising
   (self-rising) flour
5ml/1 tsp ground ginger (optional)

FOR THE DECORATION

white writer icing tube
pastel-coloured writer icing tube
selection of small multi-coloured
   sweets (candies), sugar flowers
   and silver balls

1 Put the butter and sugar in a bowl and beat together until pale and creamy. Beat in the egg and treacle, then add the flour and ginger, if using. Mix together to make a thick paste. Turn on to a lightly floured surface and knead until smooth. Wrap in clear film (plastic wrap) and chill for 30 minutes.

2 Preheat the oven to 180°C/350°F/Gas 4. Grease three baking sheets. On a piece of cardboard, draw an 11 x 8cm/41/4 x 31/4in rectangle. Add a pitched roof. Cut out the shape to use as a template. Roll out the dough on a floured surface. (It might be easier to roll out half the quantity of dough at a time.)

3 Using the template, cut out house shapes. Transfer to the baking sheets and re-roll the trimmings to make more. Bake for 12–15 minutes until risen and golden. Transfer to a wire rack to cool.

4 Use the white and pastel-coloured writer icing to pipe roof tiles, window and door frames. Secure sweets and decorations to finish.

Nutritional information per cookie: Energy 275kcal/1156kJ; Protein 4.5g; Carbohydrate 43.2g, of which sugars 12.7g; Fat 10.5g, of which saturates 6.2g; Cholesterol 44mg; Calcium 67mg; Fibre 1.2g; Sodium 79mg.

Giant birthday cookie

This giant cookie makes a fabulous alternative to the traditional birthday cake. Use chocolate chips instead of chocolate-coated raisins if you wish.

MAKES ONE 28CM/11IN COOKIE

175g/6oz/³/₄ cup unsalted
   (sweet) butter, at room
   temperature, diced
125g/4¹/₄oz/²/₃ cup light muscovado
   (brown) sugar
1 egg yolk
175g/6oz/1¹/₂ cups plain
   (all-purpose) flour
5ml/1 tsp bicarbonate of soda
   (baking soda)
finely grated rind of 1 orange
   or lemon
75g/3oz/scant 1 cup rolled oats

FOR THE DECORATION

125g/4¹/₄oz/generous ¹/₂ cup
   cream cheese
225g/8oz/2 cups icing
   (confectioners') sugar
5–10ml/1–2 tsp lemon juice
birthday candles
white and milk chocolate-coated
   raisins or peanuts
cocoa powder, for dusting
gold or silver balls, for sprinkling

1 Preheat the oven to 190°C/375°F/Gas 5. Grease a 28cm/11in metal flan tin (tart pan) and place on a large baking sheet.

2 Put the diced butter and the sugar in a large bowl and beat together until pale and creamy. Add the egg yolk to the butter mixture and stir to mix. Add the flour, bicarbonate of soda, grated orange or lemon rind and rolled oats and stir until evenly combined. Turn the mixture into the tin and flatten with a wet wooden spoon.

3 Bake for 15–20 minutes until risen and golden. Leave to cool in the tin, then carefully slide the cookie from the tin on to a large, flat plate or board.

4 To decorate, beat the cream cheese in a bowl, then add the icing sugar and 5ml/1 tsp of the lemon juice. Beat until smooth and peaking, adding more juice if required. Spoon the mixture into a piping (pastry) bag and pipe swirls around the edge of the cookie. Press the candles into the frosting. Sprinkle with chocolate raisins and dust with cocoa powder. Sprinkle with gold or silver balls.

Nutritional information per cookie: Energy 4188kcal/17559kJ; Protein 35.3g; Carbohydrate 557.4g, of which sugars 369.4g; Fat 217.5g, of which saturates 130.2g; Cholesterol 694mg; Calcium 649mg; Fibre 10.5g; Sodium 1496mg.

Mini party pizzas

These cute little cookie confections look amazingly realistic and older children will love them. They're fun to make and are simply a basic cookie topped with icing, marzipan and dark cherries.

MAKES 16

90g/3¹/₂oz/7 tbsp unsalted (sweet)
    butter, at room temperature, diced
90g/3¹/₂oz/¹/₂ cup golden caster
    (superfine) sugar
15ml/1 tbsp golden (light corn) syrup
175g/6oz/1¹/₂ cups self-raising
    (self-rising) flour

FOR THE TOPPING

150g/5oz/1¹/₄ cups icing
    (confectioners') sugar
20 –25ml/4 –5 tsp lemon juice
red food colouring
90g/3¹/₂oz yellow marzipan,
    grated (shredded)
8 dark glacé (candied) cherries, halved
a small piece of angelica, finely chopped

1 Preheat the oven to 180°C/350°F/ Gas 4. Grease two baking sheets.

2 Beat the butter and sugar together in a bowl until creamy. Beat in the syrup, then add the flour and mix to a smooth paste. Turn the mixture on to a floured surface and cut into 16 even pieces. Roll each piece into a ball, then space well apart on the baking sheets, slightly flattening each one.

3 Bake for about 12 minutes, or until pale golden. Leave on the baking sheets for 3 minutes, then transfer to a wire rack to cool.

4 For the topping, put the icing sugar in a bowl and stir in enough lemon juice to make a fairly thick, spreadable paste. Beat in enough food colouring to make the paste a deep red colour.

5 Spread the icing to within 5mm/¹/₄in of the edges of the cookies. Sprinkle with the marzipan and place a cherry in the centre. Arrange a few pieces of angelica on top so that the cookies resemble cheese and tomato pizzas.

Nutritional information per cookie: Energy 163kcal/687kJ; Protein 1.4g; Carbohydrate 28.8g, of which sugars 20.4g; Fat 5.5g, of which saturates 3g; Cholesterol 12mg; Calcium 28mg; Fibre 0.4g; Sodium 39mg.

Dolly cookies

These pretty cookies look like they belong at a doll's tea party and are great for kids to make and decorate. The cookies are very simple to make and you don't even need cookie cutters.

MAKES 24

115g/4oz/¹/₂ cup unsalted (sweet)
   butter, at room temperature, diced
50g/2oz/ ¹/₄ cup caster
   (superfine) sugar
pink food colouring
5ml/1 tsp vanilla extract
175g/6oz/1¹/₂ cups plain
   (all-purpose) flour
90g/3¹/₂oz white chocolate, broken
   into pieces
75g/3oz multi-coloured
   sweets (candies)

1 Put the butter and sugar in a bowl with a dash of pink food colouring and the vanilla extract. Beat together until smooth and creamy. Add the flour to the butter and sugar mixture and stir well until combined. Turn the dough out on to a lightly floured surface and knead until smooth.

2 Using your hands, roll the dough into a thick sausage shape, 12cm/4¹/₂in long and 5cm/2in in diameter. Wrap in clear film (plastic wrap) and chill for at least 30 minutes.

3 Preheat the oven to 180°C/350°F/Gas 4. Grease two large baking sheets. Cut the dough into 5mm/¹/₄in slices and space them apart on the baking sheets. Bake for 15–18 minutes until the cookies begin to colour. Transfer to a wire rack to cool completely.

4 Melt the chocolate in a heatproof bowl set over a pan of simmering water. Using a sharp knife, cut the sweets in half. Swirl a little chocolate on to each cookie and decorate with a ring of sweets. Leave to set.

Nutritional information per cookie: Energy 99kcal/414kJ; Protein 1.1g; Carbohydrate 12.8g, of which sugars 7.2g; Fat 5.2g, of which saturates 3.2g; Cholesterol 10.5mg; Calcium 22.8mg; Fibre 0.2g; Sodium 34.4mg.

Alphabetinis

These funny little letters are great for kids – and might even be a good way to encourage them to practise their spelling. They are a lot of fun to make and even better to eat.

MAKES ABOUT 30

2 egg whites
15ml/1 tbsp cornflour (cornstarch)
50g/2oz/1/2 cup plain (all-purpose) flour
150g/5oz/3/4 cup caster (superfine) sugar
10ml/2 tsp vanilla extract
90g/31/2oz milk chocolate

1 Preheat the oven to 180°C/350°F/ Gas 4. Line two baking sheets with baking parchment. In a bowl, whisk the egg whites into peaks. Sift the cornflour and plain flour over the egg whites and add the sugar and vanilla extract. Fold in using a large metal spoon.

2 Spoon half of the mixture into a plastic bag and squeeze it into a corner of the bag. Snip off the tip of the corner so that the cookie mixture can be squeezed out in a line, 1cm/1/2in wide.

3 Carefully, pipe letters on to one of the lined baking sheets, making each letter about 6cm/21/2in tall. Spoon the remaining cookie mixture into the bag and pipe more letters on to the second baking sheet. Bake for 12 minutes, or until crisp and golden. Transfer to a wire rack to cool.

4 Melt the chocolate in a heatproof bowl set over a pan of simmering water. Spoon the chocolate into a paper piping (pastry) bag and snip off the tip. Pipe a line of chocolate over the cookies and leave to set.

Nutritional information per cookie: Energy 42kcal/178kJ; Protein 0.5g; Carbohydrate 8.5g, of which sugars 6.9g; Fat 0.9g, of which saturates 0.6g; Cholesterol 1mg; Calcium 10mg; Fibre 0g; Sodium 8mg.

Flake "99s"

You don't need a special cutter to make these biscuits. They're shaped using an ordinary round cutter to which you add a V-shaped cone when cutting them out – simple once you've made one.

MAKES 15

150g/5oz/1¼ cups self-raising (self-rising) flour
90g/3½oz/7 tbsp unsalted (sweet) butter, diced
50g/2oz/¼ cup light muscovado (brown) sugar
1 egg yolk
5ml/1 tsp vanilla extract

FOR THE DECORATION
75g/3oz/6 tbsp unsalted (sweet) butter, softened
5ml/1 tsp vanilla extract
115g/4oz/1 cup icing (confectioners') sugar
2 chocolate flakes, cut into 5cm/2in lengths, then cut into 4 lengthways

1 Put the flour and butter in a food processor and process until mixture resembles breadcrumbs. Add the sugar, egg yolk and vanilla and blend until smooth. Wrap and chill.

2 Preheat the oven to 200°C/ 400°F/Gas 6. Grease a baking sheet. Roll the dough out thinly. Lay a 5cm/2in round cutter on the dough. Mark a point 5cm/2in away from the edge of the cutter. Cut two lines from either side of the cutter to the point, to make cornet shapes. Cut around the rest of the cutter.

3 Transfer to the baking sheet and make 14 more. Make shallow cuts 5mm/¼in apart across the cone area of each cookie. Make more cuts diagonally across the first. Bake for 8–10 minutes until golden. Leave for 2 minutes, then cool on a wire rack.

4 Beat the butter, vanilla and icing sugar until smooth. Add 5ml/1 tsp hot water and beat until light and airy. Place in a piping (pastry) bag fitted with a plain nozzle and pipe swirls onto the tops of the cookies. Push a flake piece into each biscuit.

Nutritional information per cookie: Energy 198kcal/828kJ; Protein 1.8g; Carbohydrate 23.1g, of which sugars 15.5g; Fat 11.6g, of which saturates 7.1g; Cholesterol 38mg; Calcium 38mg; Fibre 0.4g; Sodium 74mg.

Gingerbread family

You can have great fun with these cookies by creating characters with different features. By using an assortment of different gingerbread cutters you can make a gingerbread family of all shapes and sizes. To add variation, use plain or milk chocolate for decorating the cookies .

MAKES ABOUT 12

350g/12oz/3 cups plain
   (all-purpose) flour
5ml/1 tsp bicarbonate of soda
   (baking soda)
5ml/1 tsp ground ginger
115g/4oz/¹/2 cup unsalted (sweet)
   butter, chilled and diced

175g/6oz/scant 1 cup light muscovado
   (brown) sugar
1 egg
30ml/2 tbsp black treacle (molasses)
   or golden (light corn) syrup
150g/5oz white chocolate, to decorate

1 Preheat the oven to 180°C/350°F/Gas 4. Grease two large baking sheets.

2 Put the flour, bicarbonate of soda, ginger and diced butter into the food processor. Process until the mixture begins to resemble fine breadcrumbs. If necessary, scrape down the sides of the food processor bowl with a wooden spoon or spatula to remove any crumbs that have become stuck to the sides.

3 Add the sugar, egg and black treacle or golden syrup to the food processor and process the mixture until it begins to form into a ball. Turn the dough out on to a lightly floured surface, and knead until smooth and pliable.

4 Roll out the dough on a lightly floured surface (you might find it easier to roll half of the dough out at a time). Cut out figures using people-shaped cutters, then transfer to the baking sheets. Re-roll any trimmings and cut out more figures.

5 Bake for 15 minutes until slightly risen and starting to colour around the edges. Leave for 5 minutes, then transfer to a wire rack to cool.

6 To decorate, put the chocolate into a bowl. Set the bowl over a pan of simmering water and heat, stirring, until melted. Spoon the melted chocolate into paper piping (pastry) bags, snip off the tip, then pipe faces and clothes on to the cookies. Leave to set.

Nutritional information per cookie: Energy 305kcal/1281kJ; Protein 4.1g; Carbohydrate 47.6g, of which sugars 25.2g; Fat 12.2g, of which saturates 7.3g; Cholesterol 37mg; Calcium 71mg; Fibre 1.2g; Sodium 71mg.

Celebration cookies

Food and festivals go together – no matter where you are in the world, or the time of year. You cannot have a celebration without cooking something special to eat. Of course, you don't have to wait for a particular occasion – making any of the cookies in this chapter will turn an ordinary day into a festive one.

Italian glazed lemon rings

These delicately flavoured, pretty cookies look almost too good to eat. The icing contains Italian liqueur, so they are strictly for adult parties.

MAKES ABOUT 16

200g/7oz/1¾ cups self-raising
   (self-rising) flour
50g/2oz/¼ cup unsalted (sweet)
   butter, at room temperature, diced
25ml/1½ tbsp milk
50g/2oz/¼ cup caster (superfine) sugar
finely grated rind of ½ lemon
1 egg, beaten

FOR THE TOPPING

150g/5oz/1¼ cups icing
   (confectioners') sugar, sifted
30ml/2 tbsp Limoncello liqueur
15ml/1 tbsp chopped candied angelica

1 Preheat the oven to 180°C/ 350°F/Gas 4. Line two large baking sheets with baking parchment. Put the flour into a bowl and rub in the butter.

2 Put the milk, sugar and lemon rind in a small pan and stir over a low heat until the sugar has dissolved. Add to the flour mixture, together with the egg, and mix well. Knead lightly until smooth.

3 Roll walnut-size pieces of dough into strands 15cm/6in long. Twist two strands together, and join the ends to make a circle. Place on the prepared baking sheets and bake for 15–20 minutes, or until golden.

4 To make the topping, stir the icing sugar and liqueur together in a small bowl. Dip the top of each cookie into the topping and sprinkle with some chopped angelica.

Nutritional information per cookie: Energy 125kcal/530kJ; Protein 1.7g; Carbohydrate 23.5g, of which sugars 14g; Fat 3.1g, of which saturates 1.8g; Cholesterol 19mg; Calcium 28mg; Fibre 0.4g; Sodium 25mg.

Persian rice flour cookies

These prettily decorated cookies are traditionally served on special occasions with black tea. However, they taste as good with coffee or even a glass of chilled dry white wine.

MAKES ABOUT 22

75g/3oz/²/₃ cup icing (confectioners')
    sugar, sifted
225g/8oz/1 cup unsalted (sweet)
    butter, softened
300g/11oz/2¹/₂ cups rice flour
75g/3oz/²/₃ cup self-raising
    (self-rising) flour
1 egg yolk
15ml/1 tbsp rose water

FOR THE TOPPING

150g/5oz/1¹/₄ cups icing (confectioners')
    sugar, sifted
rose water
pink food colouring
crystallized rose petals or violets
    or pink sugar balls or sugar vermicelli

1 Mix together the sugar, butter, flours, egg yolk and rose water and gather into a ball. Wrap in clear film (plastic wrap) and chill. Preheat the oven to 160°C/325°F/Gas 3. Line two baking sheets with baking parchment.

2 Shape the mixture into balls. Place well apart on the prepared baking sheets and flatten each one slightly.

3 Bake for 15–20 minutes until firm but still quite pale in colour. Leave to cool on the baking sheets.

4 For the topping, put the icing sugar into a bowl and add just enough rose water to mix to a thick, flowing consistency. Add just a light touch of pink food colouring to make a very pale shade.

5 Drizzle the icing in random squiggles and circles over all the cookies. Place a few crystallized rose petals or violets or pink sugar balls on top, or sprinkle with a little sugar vermicelli. Leave to set completely before serving the cookies.

Nutritional information per cookie: Energy 180kcal/753kJ; Protein 1.4g; Carbohydrate 24.3g, of which sugars 10.8g; Fat 8.8g, of which saturates 5.4g; Cholesterol 31mg; Calcium 24mg; Fibre 0.4g; Sodium 76mg.

Chinese fortune cookies

Whether you're a rabbit or a dragon, a snake or a tiger, these charming cookies are sure to delight and are a wonderful way to celebrate the Chinese New Year with family and friends.

MAKES ABOUT 35

2 egg whites
50g/2oz/¹/₂ cup icing (confectioner's) sugar, sifted, plus extra for dusting
5ml/1 tsp almond or vanilla extract
25g/1oz/2 tbsp unsalted (sweet) butter, melted
50g/2oz/¹/₂ cup plain (all-purpose) flour
25g/1oz/¹/₃ cup desiccated (dry unsweetened shredded) coconut, lightly toasted
tiny strips of paper with "good luck", "health, wealth and happiness" and other appropriate messages typed or written on them, to decorate

1 Preheat the oven to 190°C/375°F/Gas 5. Prepare two or three sheets of baking parchment by cutting them to the size of a baking sheet. Draw two or three circles of 7.5cm/3in diameter on each sheet of parchment. Place one of these sheets of parchment on the baking sheet and set aside.

2 Put the egg whites into a clean, grease-free bowl and whisk until foamy and white. Whisk in the icing sugar, a little at a time. Beat in the almond or vanilla extract and the butter. Stir in the flour and mix lightly until smooth.

3 Place a teaspoonful of mixture into the centre of each marked circle on the parchment and spread out to fit the circle. Sprinkle with a little coconut. Bake one sheet at a time for about 5 minutes, or until light brown on the edges.

4 Loosely fold in half and place on the rim of a glass. Leave until firm, then transfer to a wire rack. Continue baking one sheet of cookies at a time. Tuck the messages into the side of each cookie. Dust very lightly with icing sugar.

Nutritional information per cookie: Energy 21kcal/87kJ; Protein 0.4g; Carbohydrate 2.7g, of which sugars 1.6g; Fat 1g, of which saturates 0.8g; Cholesterol 2mg; Calcium 3mg; Fibre 0.1g; Sodium 8mg.

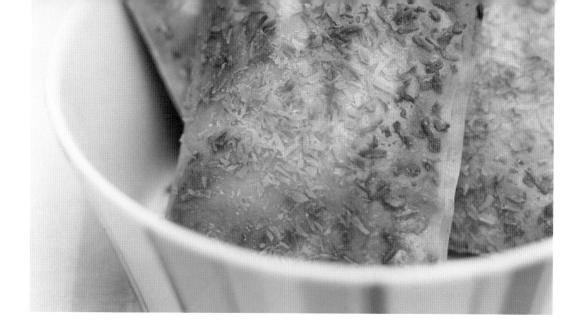

Neuris

These melt-in-the-mouth sweet and spicy samosas are traditionally eaten during the Hindu festival of Diwali and are also given as little gifts to friends and family at this time.

MAKES 12

75g/3oz/1 cup desiccated (dry
   unsweetened shredded) coconut
50g/2oz/¼ cup light muscovado
   (brown) sugar
25g/1oz/¼ cup cashew nuts, chopped
50g/2oz/⅓ cup seedless raisins
250ml/8fl oz/1 cup evaporated milk
large pinch grated nutmeg
2.5ml/½ tsp ground cinnamon
12 sheets filo pastry, about 28 x 18cm/
   11 x 7in each
sunflower oil, for brushing

FOR THE TOPPING

15ml/1 tbsp evaporated milk
15ml/1 tbsp caster (superfine) sugar
desiccated (dry unsweetened
   shredded) coconut

1 Bring the coconut, muscovado sugar, cashews, raisins and evaporated milk to the boil in a pan. Reduce the heat to low and cook for 10 minutes, stirring, until the milk has been absorbed. Stir in the spices, then leave to cool.

2 Preheat the oven to 180°C/350°F/Gas 4. Line two baking sheets with baking parchment. Brush one sheet of filo pastry with a little sunflower oil. Fold the sheet in half lengthways, then brush with more oil and fold widthways. Brush the edges of the folded pastry with water.

3 Place a spoonful of the filling on one half of the folded pastry sheet. Fold the other half of the sheet over the filling, then press to seal. Trim and place on the baking sheet. Continue until the pastry and filling have been used.

4 For the topping, heat the evaporated milk and sugar gently, stirring until the sugar has dissolved. Brush over the neuris and sprinkle with coconut. Bake for 20 minutes, until crisp and golden brown. Transfer to a wire rack and cool.

Nutritional information per cookie: Energy 164kcal/689kJ; Protein 4.2g; Carbohydrate 24.6g, of which sugars 11.6g; Fat 6.1g, of which saturates 4.1g; Cholesterol 4mg; Calcium 88mg; Fibre 1.5g; Sodium 37mg.

Simnel cookies

Enjoy these mini variations on the sweet, marzipan-covered simnel cake that is traditionally eaten at Easter and, originally, on Mothering Sunday in Britain. Children will enjoy decorating them.

MAKES ABOUT 18

175g/6oz/³⁄4 cup unsalted (sweet) butter, at room temperature, diced
115g/4oz/generous ¹⁄2 cup caster (superfine) sugar
finely grated rind of 1 lemon
2 egg yolks
225g/8oz/2 cups plain (all-purpose) flour
50g/2oz/¹⁄4 cup currants

FOR THE TOPPING

400g/14oz/³⁄4 cup marzipan
200g/7oz/1³⁄4 cups icing (confectioners') sugar, sifted
3 shades of food colouring
mini sugar-coated chocolate Easter eggs

1 Preheat the oven to 180°C/ 350°F/Gas 4. Put the butter, sugar and lemon rind in a bowl and cream until light and fluffy. Beat in the egg yolks, then stir in the flour and currants and mix to a firm dough. If it is a little soft, chill until firm.

2 Roll the dough out on a sheet of baking parchment to just under 5mm/¹⁄4in thickness. Using a 9cm/3¹⁄2in fluted cutter, stamp out rounds and place, spaced apart, on two non-stick baking sheets.

3 For the topping, roll out the marzipan to just under 5mm/¹⁄4in thickness and use a 6cm/2¹⁄2in plain or fluted cutter to stamp out the same number of rounds as there are cookies.

4 Place a marzipan round on top of each cookie and press down gently to fix the marzipan to the cookie.

5 Bake for 12 minutes, or until just golden. Remove from the oven and leave to cool on the baking sheets.

6 Put the icing sugar in a bowl and add just enough water to mix to a smooth, spreadable consistency. Divide the icing among three bowls and stir a few drops of different food colouring into each one.

7 Divide the cookies into three batches and spread each batch with icing of a different colour. While the icing is still wet, gently press a few sugar-coated eggs on top of each cookie and leave to set.

Nutritional information per cookie: Energy 285kcal/1197kJ; Protein 2.9g; Carbohydrate 45g, of which sugars 35.4g; Fat 11.6g, of which saturates 5.5g; Cholesterol 43mg; Calcium 48mg; Fibre 0.9g; Sodium 66mg.

Fourth of July blueberry softbakes

These are simply wonderful when eaten still warm from the oven. However, they are also good if allowed to cool and then packed for a traditional Independence Day picnic.

MAKES 10

150g/5oz/1¼ cups plain
(all-purpose) flour
7.5ml/1½ tsp baking powder
5ml/1 tsp ground cinnamon
50g/2oz/¼ cup unsalted (sweet) butter,
at room temperature, diced
50g/2oz/¼ cup demerara (raw) sugar,
plus extra for sprinkling
120ml/4fl oz/½ cup sour cream
90g/3½oz/1 cup fresh blueberries
50g/2oz/½ cup semi-dried cranberries

1 Preheat the oven to 190°C/ 375°F/Gas 5. Line two baking sheets with baking parchment. Sift together the flour, baking powder and cinnamon into a large bowl.

2 Add the diced butter and rub in with your fingers until the mixture resembles fine breadcrumbs. Stir in the demerara sugar.

3 Add the sour cream, blueberries and cranberries and stir until just combined. Spoon ten mounds of the mixture, spaced well apart, on to the prepared baking sheets.

4 Sprinkle with the extra demerara sugar and bake for 20 minutes, or until golden and firm in the centre. Serve warm.

Nutritional information per cookie: Energy 185kcal/775kJ; Protein 3.3g; Carbohydrate 25.2g, of which sugars 9.8g; Fat 8.4g, of which saturates 4.6g; Cholesterol 78mg; Calcium 48mg; Fibre 0.8g; Sodium 42mg.

Christmas tree angels

Why not make these charming edible decorations to brighten your Yuletide? However, don't hang them on the tree until Christmas Eve or they'll all be gone by Christmas Day.

MAKES 20–30

90g/3^1/2oz/scant ^{1}/2 cup demerara
    (raw) sugar
200g/7oz/scant 1 cup golden
    (light corn) syrup
5ml/1 tsp ground ginger
5ml/1 tsp ground cinnamon
1.5ml/^{1}/4 tsp ground cloves
115g/4oz/^{1}/2 cup unsalted (sweet)
    butter, cut into pieces
10ml/2 tsp bicarbonate of soda
    (baking soda)

1 egg, beaten
500g/1^1/4lb/4^1/2 cups plain
    (all-purpose) flour, sifted

FOR THE DECORATION
1 egg white
175–225g/6–8oz/1^1/2–2 cups icing
    (confectioners') sugar, sifted
silver and gold balls
fine ribbon

1 Preheat the oven to 160°C/325°F/Gas 3. Line two baking sheets with baking parchment. Bring the sugar, syrup, ginger, cinnamon and cloves to the boil over a low heat, stirring constantly. Remove from the heat.

2 Put the butter in a bowl and pour over the sugar mixture. Add the bicarbonate of soda and stir until the butter has melted. Beat in the egg, then stir in the flour. Mix, then knead to form a dough.

3 Divide the dough into four pieces and roll out, one at a time, between sheets of baking parchment, to a thickness of 3mm/^{1}/8in. To make simple angels, stamp out rounds of dough using a plain cutter. Cut off two segments from either side of the round to give a body and two wings. Place the wings, rounded side facing down, behind the body and press together.

4 Roll a small piece of dough for the head, place at the top of the body and flatten. Using a skewer, make a wide hole in the cookies through which ribbon can be threaded. Place on the baking sheets. Bake for 10–15 minutes until golden brown. Transfer to a wire rack to cool.

5 For the decoration, beat the egg white with a fork. Whisk in icing sugar until you have a soft-peak consistency. Put the icing in a piping (pastry) bag fitted with a writing nozzle and decorate the cookies. Add silver and gold balls. Finally, thread ribbon through the holes in the cookies.

Nutritional information per cookie: Energy 147kcal/622kJ; Protein 1.9g; Carbohydrate 28.7g, of which sugars 16g; Fat 3.6g, of which saturates 2.1g; Cholesterol 15mg; Calcium 31mg; Fibre 0.5g; Sodium 45mg.

Spicy hearts and stars

These soft cookies have a wonderfully chewy texture and a deliciously warm, fragrant flavour.
Serve with coffee at the end of a festive meal, or make them as a gift on a special occasion.

MAKES ABOUT 25

115g/4oz/¹/₂ cup unsalted (sweet)
   butter, softened
115g/4oz/generous ¹/₂ cup light
   muscovado (brown) sugar
1 egg
50g/2oz/1¹/₂ tbsp golden
   (light corn) syrup
50g/2oz/1¹/₂ tbsp black treacle (molasses)
400g/14oz/3¹/₂ cups self-raising
   (self-rising) flour
10ml/2 tsp ground ginger

FOR THE TOPPINGS

200g/7oz plain (semisweet) or
   milk chocolate
150g/5oz/1¹/₄ cups icing (confectioners')
   sugar, sifted

1 Beat together the butter and sugar until creamy. Beat in the egg, syrup and treacle together. Sift in the flour and ginger and mix to form a firm dough. Chill for 20 minutes. Meanwhile, preheat the oven to 180°C/350°F/Gas 4 and line two large baking sheets with a layer of baking parchment.

2 Roll out the dough on a lightly floured surface to just under 1cm/¹/₂in thick and use biscuit (cookie) cutters to stamp out heart and star shapes. Place, spaced slightly apart, on the prepared baking sheets and bake for about 10 minutes, or until risen. Cool on a wire rack.

3 To make the toppings, melt the chocolate in a microwave or in a heatproof bowl set over a pan of barely simmering water. Use the melted chocolate to coat the heart-shaped cookies. Put the icing sugar into a bowl and mix with enough warm water to make a coating consistency, then use this to glaze the star-shaped cookies.

Nutritional information per cookie: Energy 185kcal/781kJ; Protein 2.3g; Carbohydrate 31.5g, of which sugars 19.3g; Fat 6.5g, of which saturates 3.8g; Cholesterol 18mg; Calcium 44mg; Fibre 0.7g; Sodium 41mg.

Kourabiedes

Lightly spiced and delicately flavoured, these crisp little crescents originally come from Greece and are perfect for parties and festive occasions such as christenings and weddings.

MAKES ABOUT 20

115g/4oz/¹⁄₂ cup unsalted (sweet) butter, softened
pinch of ground nutmeg
10ml/2 tsp orange flower water
50g/2oz/¹⁄₂ cup icing (confectioners') sugar, plus extra for dusting
90g/3¹⁄₂oz/³⁄₄ cup plain (all-purpose) flour
115g/4oz/1 cup ground almonds
25g/1oz/¹⁄₄ cup whole almonds, toasted and chopped

1 Preheat the oven to 160°C/325°F/Gas 3. Line two large baking sheets with baking parchment. Beat the butter in a large bowl until soft and creamy.

2 Beat in the nutmeg and orange flower water. Add the icing sugar and beat until fluffy.

3 Add the flour, ground and chopped almonds and mix well, then use your hands to bring the mixture together to form a dough, being careful not to overwork it.

4 Shape pieces of dough into sausages about 7.5cm/3in long. Curve each one into a crescent shape and place, spaced well apart, on the prepared baking sheets. Bake for about 15 minutes, or until firm but still pale in colour. Cool for about 5 minutes, then dust with a little icing sugar.

Nutritional information per cookie: Energy 111kcal/461kJ; Protein 1.9g; Carbohydrate 6.6g, of which sugars 3g; Fat 8.7g, of which saturates 3.3g; Cholesterol 12mg; Calcium 25mg; Fibre 0.7g; Sodium 36mg.

Sweet hearts

These cookies are for Valentine's Day or an anniversary, but you could use different-shaped cutters in the same way to make cookies for other occasions – stars and bells for Christmas, perhaps, or fluted "flowers" for a special birthday or Mother's Day present.

MAKES 12–14

50g/2oz/¼ cup unsalted (sweet) butter, softened

75g/3oz/scant ½ cup caster (superfine) sugar

1 egg yolk

150g/5oz/1¼ cups plain (all-purpose) flour

25g/1oz dark (bittersweet) chocolate, melted and cooled

25–50g/1–2oz dark (bittersweet) chocolate, to decorate

1 Preheat the oven to 180°C/350°F/Gas 4. Line two baking sheets with baking parchment. Put the butter, sugar and egg yolk in a bowl and beat well. Stir in the flour and then knead until smooth.

2 Divide the dough in half, then knead the melted chocolate into one half until it is evenly coloured. Roll out the chocolate dough between two sheets of baking parchment, to a thickness of about 3mm/⅛in. Then roll out the plain dough in the same way. Cut out hearts from both doughs using a 7.5cm/3in biscuit (cookie) cutter. Place the hearts on the prepared baking sheets.

3 Using a smaller heart-shaped cutter, stamp out the centres from all the hearts. Place a light-coloured heart in the centre of a larger chocolate heart and vice versa. Bake the cookies for about 10 minutes, or until just beginning to turn brown. Remove from the oven and leave to cool.

4 To decorate, melt the chocolate in a microwave or in a heatproof bowl set over a pan of hot water. Put into a disposable piping (pastry) bag. Leave the chocolate to cool slightly.

5 Snip the end off the piping bag and carefully pipe dots directly onto the outer part of the large chocolate hearts (with the plain centres). Then pipe zigzags on the pale part of the large plain hearts (with the chocolate centres). Put the cookies aside in a cool place and leave until they are set.

Nutritional information per cookie: Energy 107kcal/449kJ; Protein 1.4g; Carbohydrate 16.2g, of which sugars 8g; Fat 4.5g, of which saturates 2.6g; Cholesterol 22mg; Calcium 21mg; Fibre 0.4g; Sodium 23mg.

Rugelach

Jewish cookies, traditionally served during the eight-day festival of Hanukkah, these little crescents have a spicy fruit-and-nut filling. They can be enjoyed at any time of the year.

MAKES ABOUT 24

115g/4oz/1/2 cup unsalted (sweet)
   butter, chilled and diced
115g/4oz/1/2 cup cream cheese
120ml/4fl oz/1/2 cup sour cream
250g/9oz/21/4 cups plain
   (all-purpose) flour
beaten egg, to glaze

FOR THE FILLING

50g/2oz/1/4 cup caster
   (superfine) sugar
10ml/2 tsp ground cinnamon
60ml/4 tbsp raisins, chopped
60ml/4 tbsp ready-to-eat dried
   apricots, chopped
75g/3oz/3/4 cup walnuts, finely chopped

1 To make the dough, put the butter, cream cheese and sour cream into a food processor and process until just creamy and combined. Add the flour and process briefly, until the mixture just comes together, taking care not to overmix. Remove, wrap in clear film (plastic wrap) and chill for 6 hours.

2 Preheat the oven to 180°C/350°F/Gas 4. Line two large baking sheets with baking parchment. For the filling, mix all the filling ingredients together.

3 Divide the dough into four. Take one piece and leave the rest in the refrigerator, as it is important to keep the dough as cold as possible because it is very sticky and therefore difficult to roll out. Sprinkle a sheet of baking parchment with flour and quickly roll out the dough to a round as thin as possible. Cut into six wedges; sprinkle with a quarter of the filling.

4 Starting at the wide end, roll each triangle up towards the point. Curve each roll into a crescent and place, the pointed side down, on the baking sheets. Repeat with the remaining dough and filling. Brush with beaten egg and bake for 15–20 minutes until golden. Leave to cool on a wire rack.

Nutritional information per cookie: Energy 143kcal/596kJ; Protein 1.9g; Carbohydrate 13.2g, of which sugars 5.3g; Fat 9.5g, of which saturates 4.7g; Cholesterol 18mg; Calcium 32mg; Fibre 0.6g; Sodium 48mg.

Oznei haman

These little cookies, shaped like tricorns – three-cornered hats – are eaten at the Jewish feast called Purim, which celebrates the Jews' deliverance from the scheming Haman.

MAKES ABOUT 20

115g/4oz/¹/₂ cup unsalted (sweet)
   butter, at room temperature, diced
115g/4oz/generous ¹/₂ cup caster
   (superfine) sugar
2.5ml/¹/₂ tsp vanilla extract
3 egg yolks
250g/9oz/2¹/₄ cups plain
   (all-purpose) flour
beaten egg to seal and glaze

FOR THE FILLING

40g/1¹/₂oz/3 tbsp poppy seeds
15ml/1 tbsp clear honey
25g/1oz/2 tbsp caster (superfine) sugar
finely grated rind of 1 lemon
15ml/1 tbsp lemon juice
40g/1¹/₂oz/¹/₃ cup ground almonds
1 small (US medium) egg, beaten
25g/1oz/scant ¹/₄ cup raisins

1 Beat the butter with the sugar until light and creamy. Beat in the vanilla and egg yolks. Sift over the flour, stir in, then work into a dough with your hands. Knead until smooth. Wrap and chill.

2 For the filling, put the poppy seeds, honey, sugar, lemon rind and juice into a pan with 60ml/4 tbsp water and bring to the boil, stirring. Remove from the heat and beat in the almonds, egg and raisins. Cool.

3 Preheat the oven to 180°C/350°F/Gas 4. Line two large baking sheets with baking parchment. Roll out the dough on a lightly floured surface to 3mm/¹/₈in thickness. Using a plain round 7.5cm/3in cutter, stamp out rounds. Place a heaped teaspoon of filling on each round. Brush the edges with beaten egg, then bring the sides to the centre to form a tricorn shape. Seal the edges well together and place on the prepared baking sheets, spaced slightly apart.

4 Brush with beaten egg and bake for 20–30 minutes, or until golden brown. Transfer to a wire rack and leave to cool.

Nutritional information per cookie: Energy 156kcal/653kJ; Protein 2.8g; Carbohydrate 18.7g, of which sugars 9.1g; Fat 8.3g, of which saturates 3.6g; Cholesterol 52mg; Calcium 46mg; Fibre 0.7g; Sodium 42mg.

Chocolate cookies

This has to be a favourite chapter for almost everyone – chocolate cookies are universally popular, loved by young and old alike. This is hardly surprising, with such mouthwatering recipes as Chocolate Florentines, Giant Triple Chocolate Cookies, Rich Chocolate Cookie Slice and Mini Chocolate Marylands.

Rich chocolate cookie slice

These rich, dark chocolate refrigerator cookies are perfect served with strong coffee, either as a mid-morning treat or even in place of dessert. They are always very popular.

MAKES ABOUT 10

275g/10oz fruit and nut plain (semisweet) chocolate
130g/4¹/₂oz/generous¹/₂ cup unsalted (sweet) butter, diced
90g/3¹/₂oz digestive biscuits (graham crackers)
90g/3¹/₂oz white chocolate

1 Grease and line the base and sides of a 450g/1lb loaf tin (pan) with baking parchment. Break the fruit and nut chocolate into even pieces and place in a heatproof bowl along with the diced unsalted butter.

2 Set the bowl over a pan of simmering water and stir gently until melted. Cool for 20 minutes.

3 Break the digestive biscuits into small pieces with your fingers. Finely chop the white chocolate. Stir the broken biscuits and white chocolate into the cooled, melted fruit and nut chocolate until combined. Turn the mixture into the prepared tin and pack down gently. Chill for 2 hours, or until set.

4 To serve, turn out the mixture and remove the lining paper. Cut into slices with a sharp knife.

Nutritional information per cookie: Energy 326kcal/1361kJ; Protein 2.7g; Carbohydrate 29g, of which sugars 23.8g; Fat 23g, of which saturates 13.9g; Cholesterol 33mg; Calcium 44mg; Fibre 0.9g; Sodium 144mg.

Giant triple chocolate cookies

Here is the ultimate cookie, packed full of chocolate and macadamia nuts. You will have to be patient when they come out of the oven, as they are too soft to move until completely cold.

MAKES 12 LARGE COOKIES

90g/3¹/₂oz milk chocolate
90g/3¹/₂oz white chocolate
300g/11oz dark (bittersweet) chocolate
    (minimum 70 per cent cocoa solids)
90g/3¹/₂oz/7 tbsp unsalted (sweet)
    butter, at room temperature, diced
5ml/1 tsp vanilla extract
150g/5oz/³/₄ cup light muscovado
    (brown) sugar
150g/5oz/1¹/₄ cups self-raising
    (self-rising) flour
100g/3³/₄oz/scant 1 cup macadamia
    nut halves

1 Preheat the oven to 180°C/350°F/Gas 4. Line two baking sheets with baking parchment. Coarsely chop the milk and white chocolate and put them in a bowl.

2 Chop 200g/7oz of the dark chocolate into very large chunks, at least 2cm/³/₄in in size. Set aside.

3 Break up the remaining dark chocolate and place in a heatproof bowl set over a pan of barely simmering water. Stir until melted and smooth. Remove from the heat and stir in the butter, then the vanilla extract and muscovado sugar.

4 Add the flour and mix gently. Add half the dark chocolate chunks, all the milk and white chocolate and the nuts and fold together.

5 Spoon 12 mounds on to the baking sheets. Press the remaining dark chocolate chunks into the top of each cookie. Bake for about 12 minutes until just beginning to colour. Cool on the baking sheets.

Nutritional information per cookie: Energy 416kcal/1738kJ; Protein 4.3g; Carbohydrate 47.6g, of which sugars 37.8g; Fat 24.4g, of which saturates 11.8g; Cholesterol 21mg; Calcium 71mg; Fibre 1.6g; Sodium 84mg.

Chocolate wands

Shaping these long, wafery chocolate cookies is fun, but you need to work quickly so it might take a few attempts to get the technique just right. Only bake two cookies at a time; any more and they will become brittle before you have time to shape them into wands.

MAKES 10–12

3 egg whites
90g/3¹/₂oz/ ¹/₂ cup caster
   (superfine) sugar
25g/1oz/2 tbsp unsalted (sweet)
   butter, melted
30ml/2 tbsp plain (all-purpose) flour

15ml/1 tbsp unsweetened
   cocoa powder
30ml/2 tbsp single (light) cream
90g/3¹/₂oz milk chocolate, broken
   into pieces and multi-coloured
   sprinkles, to decorate

1 Preheat the oven to 180°C/350°F/Gas 4. Line two large baking sheets with baking parchment and grease the paper well. In a bowl, briefly beat together the egg whites and sugar until the whites are broken up. Add the melted butter, flour, cocoa powder and cream to the egg whites and beat with a wooden spoon until smooth.

2 Place 2 teaspoons of the mixture to one side of a baking sheet and spread the mixture into an oval shape, about 15cm/6in long. Spoon more mixture on to the other side of the baking sheet and shape in the same way.

3 Bake for 7–8 minutes until the edges begin to darken. Meanwhile, prepare two more cookies on the second baking sheet so you can put them in the oven while shaping the first batch into wands.

4 Leave the cookies on the paper for 30 seconds, then lift one off and wrap it around the handle of a wooden spoon. As soon as it starts to hold its shape ease it off the spoon and shape the second cookie in the same way. Continue baking and shaping the cookies until all the mixture has been used up.

5 Melt the chocolate in a heatproof bowl set over a pan of simmering water. Heat, stirring occasionally, until the chocolate has melted. Dip the ends of the cookies in the chocolate, turning them until the ends are thickly coated.

6 Sprinkle the chocolate-coated ends of the cookies with sprinkles and place on a sheet of baking parchment. Leave for about 1 hour to set.

Nutritional information per cookie: Energy 103kcal/432kJ; Protein 1.6g; Carbohydrate 14.3g, of which sugars 12.2g; Fat 4.8g, of which saturates 2.9g; Cholesterol 8mg; Calcium 28mg; Fibre 0.3g; Sodium 41mg.

Mini chocolate Marylands

These tasty little cookies are perfect for any age group. They're easy to make and even young children can get involved with helping to press the chocolate chips into the unbaked dough.

MAKES 40–45

125g/4¼oz/generous ½ cup
   unsalted (sweet) butter, at room
   temperature, diced
90g/3½oz/½ cup caster
   (superfine) sugar
1 egg
1 egg yolk
5ml/1 tsp vanilla extract
175g/6oz/1½ cups self-raising
   (self-rising) flour
125ml/4½fl oz/ generous ½ cup milk
90g/3½oz/generous ½ cup
   chocolate chips

1 Preheat the oven to 180°C/ 350°F/Gas 4. Grease two large baking sheets.

2 Beat the butter and sugar together in a large bowl until pale and creamy.

3 Add the egg, egg yolk, vanilla extract, flour, milk and half of the chocolate chips to the bowl and stir well until the mixture is thoroughly combined.

4 Using two teaspoons, place small mounds of the mixture on the baking sheets, spacing them apart.

5 Press the remaining chocolate chips on to the mounds of cookie dough and press down gently.

6 Bake for 10–15 minutes until pale golden. Leave the cookies on the baking sheet for 2 minutes to firm up, then transfer to a wire rack to cool completely.

Nutritional information per cookie: Energy 54kcal/227kJ; Protein 0.7g; Carbohydrate 6.4g, of which sugars 3.5g; Fat 3g, of which saturates 1.8g; Cholesterol 10mg; Calcium 19mg; Fibre 0.2g; Sodium 33mg.

Chocolate whirls

These cookies are so easy that you don't even have to make any dough. They're made with ready-made puff pastry rolled up with a chocolate filling. They're great as a special treat for breakfast.

MAKES ABOUT 20

75g/3oz/¹/₃ cup golden caster (superfine) sugar
40g/1¹/₂oz/6 tbsp unsweetened cocoa powder
2 eggs
500g/1lb 2oz puff pastry
25g/1oz/2 tbsp butter, softened
75g/3oz/generous ¹/₂ cup sultanas (golden raisins)
90g/3¹/₂oz milk chocolate, broken into pieces

1 Preheat the oven to 220°C/ 425°F/Gas 7. Grease two large baking sheets.

2 Put the sugar, cocoa powder and eggs in a bowl and mix to a paste.

3 Roll out the pastry on a lightly floured surface to make a 30cm/12in square. Trim off any rough edges using a sharp knife.

4 Dot the pastry all over with the softened butter, then spread with the chocolate paste and sprinkle the sultanas over the top.

5 Roll the pastry into a sausage-shape, then cut the roll into 1cm/ ¹/₂in slices. Place the slices on the baking sheets, spacing them apart.

6 Bake for 10 minutes until risen and pale golden. Transfer to a wire rack and leave to cool.

7 Melt the chocolate over a pan of simmering water.

8 Spoon or pipe lines of melted chocolate over the cookies, taking care not to completely hide the swirls of chocolate filling.

Nutritional information per cookie: Energy 165kcal/689kJ; Protein 2.9g; Carbohydrate 18.6g, of which sugars 9.4g; Fat 9.5g, of which saturates 1.9g; Cholesterol 23mg; Calcium 34mg; Fibre 0.4g; Sodium 117mg.

Chocolate box cookies

These prettily decorated, bitesize cookies look as though they've come straight out of a box of chocolates. They're great for a special tea or for wrapping as gifts.

MAKES ABOUT 50

175g/6oz/1¹/₂ cups self-raising
   (self-rising) flour
25g/1oz/¹/₄ cup unsweetened
   cocoa powder
5ml/1 tsp mixed (apple pie) spice
50g/2oz/¹/₄ cup unsalted (sweet)
   butter, at room temperature, diced
115g/4oz/generous ¹/₂ cup caster
   (superfine) sugar
1 egg, plus 1 egg yolk

FOR THE DECORATION

150g/5oz milk chocolate
150g/5oz white chocolate
100g/3³/₄oz plain (semisweet) chocolate
whole almonds or walnuts
cocoa powder, for dusting

1 Grease two baking sheets. Put the flour, cocoa, spice and butter into a food processor and process until blended. Add the sugar, egg and egg yolk and mix until smooth. Turn the dough out on to a floured surface and knead. Cut the dough in half and roll out to form two logs, each 33cm/13in long. Cut each log into 1cm/¹/₂in slices. Place on the baking sheets, and chill for 30 minutes.

2 Preheat the oven to 180°C/350°F/Gas 4. Bake for 10 minutes until slightly risen, then transfer to a wire rack to cool. Break the chocolate into three heatproof bowls and melt separately over a pan of simmering water. Divide the cookies into six batches.

3 Using a fork, dip one batch, a cookie at a time, into the milk chocolate to coat completely. Place on baking parchment. Taking the next batch of cookies, half-dip in milk chocolate and place on baking parchment.

4 Continue with the next two batches of cookies and the white chocolate. Completely coat one batch, then half-coat the second. Continue with the remaining cookies, completely coating one batch in the plain chocolate and half-dipping the other. Press a nut on to the the plain chocolate-coated cookies.

5 Put the leftover white chocolate in a plastic bag and squeeze it into one corner. Snip off the tip, then drizzle chocolate over the milk chocolate-coated cookies. Dust the white chocolate-coated cookies with cocoa powder.

Nutritional information per cookie: Energy 74kcal/312kJ; Protein 1.2g; Carbohydrate 9.9g, of which sugars 7.2g; Fat 3.6g, of which saturates 2.1g; Cholesterol 11mg; Calcium 23mg; Fibre 0.2g; Sodium 19mg.

Chocolate florentines

These big, flat, crunchy cookies are just like traditional florentines but use tiny seeds instead of nuts. Rolling the edges in milk or white chocolate makes them feel like a real treat.

MAKES 12

50g/2oz/¼ cup unsalted (sweet) butter
50g/2oz/¼ cup caster (superfine) sugar
15ml/1 tbsp milk
25g/1oz/scant ¼ cup pumpkin seeds
40g/1½oz/generous ¼ cup
   sunflower seeds
50g/2oz/scant ½ cup raisins
25g/1oz/2 tbsp multi-coloured glacé
   (candied) cherries, chopped
30ml/2 tbsp plain (all-purpose) flour
125g/4¼oz milk or white chocolate

1 Preheat the oven to 180°C/350°F/Gas 4. Line two baking sheets with baking parchment and grease the paper well.

2 Melt the butter with the sugar, stirring, until the sugar has dissolved, then cook until bubbling. Remove the pan from the heat and stir in the milk, pumpkin and sunflower seeds, raisins, glacé cherries and flour. Mix well.

3 Spoon 6 teaspoonfuls of the mixture on to each baking sheet, spacing them apart. Bake for 8–10 minutes until the cookies are turning dark golden. Using a metal spatula, push back the edges of the cookies to neaten. Leave for 5 minutes to firm up, then transfer to a wire rack to cool.

4 Break up the chocolate and put in a heatproof bowl set over a pan of simmering water. Heat, stirring frequently, until melted. Roll the edges of the cookies in the chocolate and leave to set on a sheet of baking parchment for about 1 hour.

Nutritional information per cookie: Energy 157kcal/656kJ; Protein 2.2g; Carbohydrate 17.5g, of which sugars 14.8g; Fat 9.1g, of which saturates 4.3g; Cholesterol 11mg; Calcium 40mg; Fibre 0.6g; Sodium 38mg.

Chocolate cookies on sticks

Let your imagination run riot when decorating these fun chocolate cookies. Use plenty of brightly coloured sweets or create a real chocolate feast by only using chocolate decorations.

MAKES 12

125g/4¹/₄oz milk chocolate, broken
    into pieces
75g/3oz white chocolate, broken
    into pieces
50g/2oz chocolate-coated
    sweetmeal cookies, crumbled
    into chunks
a selection of small coloured sweets
    (candies), chocolate chips
    or chocolate-coated raisins
12 wooden ice lolly
    (popsicle) sticks

1 Melt the milk and white chocolate separately in a heatproof bowl set over a pan of hot water. Draw six 7cm/2³/₄in rounds on baking parchment and six 9 x 7cm/3¹/₂ x 2³/₄in rectangles. Invert the paper on to a large tray.

2 Spoon the milk chocolate into the outlines on the paper, reserving a spoonful of chocolate. Spread the chocolate to the edges.

3 Press the end of a wooden ice lolly stick into each of the shapes, and spoon over a little more melted milk chocolate to cover the stick. Sprinkle the chocolate shapes with the crumbled cookies.

4 Drizzle the cookies with the white chocolate, then sprinkle the cookies with the sweets, chocolate chips or chocolate raisins, pressing them to make sure they stick. Chill for about 1 hour until set, then peel away the paper.

Nutritional information per cookie: Energy 107kcal/448kJ; Protein 1.5g; Carbohydrate 12.3g, of which sugars 10.9g; Fat 6.1g, of which saturates 3.5g; Cholesterol 2mg; Calcium 43mg; Fibre 0.2g; Sodium 30mg.

Marbled caramel chocolate slice

The classic millionaire's slice gets its name from the rich combination of ingredients. It is made even more special here with a decorative and tasty marbled chocolate topping.

MAKES ABOUT 24

FOR THE BASE
250g/9oz/2¼ cups plain (all-purpose) flour
75g/3oz/½ cup caster (superfine) sugar
175g/6oz/¾ cup unsalted (sweet) butter, softened

FOR THE FILLING
90g/3½oz/7 tbsp unsalted (sweet) butter, diced

90g/3½oz/scant ½ cup light muscovado (brown) sugar
2 x 397g/14oz cans sweetened condensed milk

FOR THE TOPPING
90g/3½oz plain (semisweet) chocolate
90g/3½oz milk chocolate
50g/2oz white chocolate

1 Preheat the oven to 180°C/350°F/Gas 4. Line and lightly grease a 33 x 23cm/13 x 9in Swiss roll tin (jelly roll pan). Put the flour and caster sugar in a bowl and rub in the butter until the mixture resembles fine breadcrumbs. Work with your hands until the mixture forms a dough.

2 Put the dough into the prepared tin and press it out with your hand to cover the base. Use the back of a tablespoon to smooth it evenly into the tin. Prick all over with a fork and bake for about 20 minutes, or until firm to the touch and very light brown. Set aside and leave in the tin to cool.

3 For the filling, put the butter, muscovado sugar and condensed milk into a pan and heat gently, stirring, until the sugar has dissolved. Stirring constantly, bring to the boil. Reduce the heat and simmer very gently, stirring, for 5–10 minutes, or until it has thickened and has turned a caramel colour. Remove from the heat.

4 Pour the filling mixture over the cookie base, spread evenly, then leave until cold.

5 For the topping, melt each type of chocolate separately in a heatproof bowl set over a pan of hot water. Spoon lines of plain and milk chocolate over the set caramel filling. Add small spoonfuls of white chocolate. Use a skewer to form a marbled effect on the topping.

Nutritional information per cookie: Energy 305kcal/1281kJ; Protein 4.6g; Carbohydrate 39.6g, of which sugars 31.6g; Fat 15.4g, of which saturates 9.6g; Cholesterol 37mg; Calcium 132mg; Fibre 0.4g; Sodium 120mg.

Chocolate caramel nuggets

Inside each of these buttery cookies lies a soft-centred chocolate-coated caramel. The nuggets are at their most delicious served an hour or so after baking.

MAKES 14

150g/5oz/1¼ cups self-raising (self-rising) flour
90g/3½oz/7 tbsp unsalted (sweet) butter, chilled and diced
50g/2oz/ ¼ cup golden caster (superfine) sugar
1 egg yolk
5ml/1 tsp vanilla extract
14 soft-centred chocolate caramels
icing (confectioners') sugar and unsweetened cocoa powder, for dusting

1 Put the flour and diced butter in a food processor and process until the mixture resembles breadcrumbs.

2 Add the sugar, egg yolk and vanilla extract to the food processor and process to a smooth dough. Wrap the dough in clear film (plastic wrap) and chill for 30 minutes.

3 Preheat the oven to 200°C/400°F/Gas 6. Grease a large baking sheet.

4 Roll out the dough thinly on a lightly floured surface and cut out 28 rounds using a 5cm/2in cutter.

5 Place one chocolate caramel on a cookie round, then lay a second round on top. Pinch the edges of the dough together so that the chocolate caramel is completely enclosed, then place on the baking sheet.

6 Make the remaining cookies in the same way. Bake for about 10 minutes until pale golden.

7 Transfer the cookies to a wire rack and leave to cool completely.

8 Serve lightly dusted with icing sugar and cocoa powder.

Nutritional information per cookie: Energy 149kcal/625kJ; Protein 1.8g; Carbohydrate 18.7g, of which sugars 9.5g; Fat 8g, of which saturates 4.6g; Cholesterol 30mg; Calcium 34mg; Fibre 0.3g; Sodium 58mg.

Fruity chocolate cookie-cakes

The combination of spongy cookie, fruity preserve and dark chocolate makes irresistible eating for kids of all ages. As cookies go, these are a little fiddly, but that's all part of the fun.

MAKES 18

90g/3¹/₂oz/¹/₂ cup caster
   (superfine) sugar
2 eggs
50g/2oz/¹/₂ cup plain (all-purpose) flour
75g/3oz/6 tbsp apricot-orange
   marmalade or apricot jam
125g/4¹/₄oz plain (semisweet) chocolate

1 Preheat the oven to 190°C/ 375°F/Gas 5. Grease 18 patty tins (muffin pans), preferably non-stick. (You may need to bake the cookies in batches.)

2 Stand a mixing bowl in very hot water for 2 minutes to heat through, keeping the inside of the bowl dry. Put the sugar and eggs in the bowl and whisk until light and frothy and the beaters leave a ribbon trail when lifted. Sift the flour over the mixture and stir in using a metal spoon.

3 Divide mixture among the tins. Bake for 10 minutes until firm and golden at the edges. Lift from tins and transfer to a wire rack to cool.

4 Press the marmalade or jam through a sieve (strainer). Spoon a little of the jam on to the centre of each cookie.

5 Break the chocolate into pieces and place in a heatproof bowl set over a pan of gently simmering water. Heat, stirring frequently, until melted and smooth.

6 Spoon a little of the chocolate on to the top of each cookie and spread gently to the edges with a metal spatula. Once the chocolate has just started to set, very gently press it with the back of a fork to give a textured surface. Leave the cookies to set for at least 1 hour before serving.

Nutritional information per cookie: Energy 84kcal/353kJ; Protein 1.3g; Carbohydrate 14.7g, of which sugars 12.5g; Fat 2.6g, of which saturates 1.3g; Cholesterol 22mg; Calcium 12mg; Fibre 0.3g; Sodium 11mg.

Chocolate thumbprint cookies

Chunky, chocolatey and gooey all at the same time, these gorgeous cookies are filled with a spoonful of chocolate spread after baking to really add to their indulgent feel.

MAKES 16

115g/4oz/1/2 cup unsalted (sweet) butter, at room temperature, diced

115g/4oz/generous 1/2 cup light muscovado (brown) sugar

1 egg

75g/3oz/2/3 cup plain (all-purpose) flour

25g/1oz/1/4 cup unsweetened cocoa powder

2.5ml/1/2 tsp bicarbonate of soda (baking soda)

115g/4oz/generous 1 cup rolled oats

75–90ml/5–6 tbsp chocolate spread

1 Preheat the oven to 180°C/350°F/Gas 4. Grease a large baking sheet. In a bowl, beat together the butter and sugar until creamy.

2 Add the egg, flour, cocoa powder, bicarbonate of soda and rolled oats to the bowl and mix well.

3 Roll spoonfuls of the mixture into balls. Place the balls on the baking sheet, spaced apart. Flatten slightly.

4 Dip a thumb in flour and press into the centre of each cookie to make an indent.

5 Bake the cookies in the oven for 10 minutes. Leave for 2 minutes to firm up slightly, then carefully transfer the cookies to a wire rack to cool completely.

6 Spoon a little chocolate spread into the centre of each cookie.

Nutritional information per cookie: Energy 163kcal/682kJ; Protein 2.3g; Carbohydrate 19.3g, of which sugars 10.3g; Fat 9g, of which saturates 4.1g; Cholesterol 27mg; Calcium 19mg; Fibre 0.8g; Sodium 66mg.

Triple chocolate sandwiches

Chocolate shortbread is a brilliant base for sandwiching or coating in melted chocolate. Kids of any age can enjoy making them as they don't need to be perfectly uniform.

MAKES 15

125g/4¼oz/generous ½ cup unsalted
   (sweet) butter, chilled and diced
150g/5oz/1¼ cups plain
   (all-purpose) flour
30ml/2 tbsp unsweetened cocoa powder
50g/2oz/¼ cup caster (superfine) sugar
75g/3oz white chocolate, broken
   into pieces
25g/1oz/2 tbsp unsalted (sweet) butter
115g/4oz milk chocolate, broken
   into pieces

1 Put the butter, flour and cocoa in a food processor. Process until the mixture resembles breadcrumbs. Add the sugar and process again until the mixture forms a dough. Transfer to a clean surface and knead lightly. Wrap in clear film (plastic wrap) and chill for 30 minutes.

2 Preheat the oven to 200°C/ 400°F/Gas 6. Grease a baking sheet. Roll out the chilled dough on a floured surface to a 33 x 16cm/13 x 6¼in rectangle. Lift on to the baking sheet and trim the edges. Cut the dough in half lengthways, then cut across at 2cm/¾in intervals to make 30 small bars.

3 Prick each bar with a fork and bake for 12–15 minutes until just dark around the edges. Cut between the bars while still warm. Leave for 2 minutes, then cool on a wire rack.

4 For the filling, melt the white chocolate and half the butter in a heatproof bowl set over a pan of simmering water. Spread a little filling on to one of the bars. Place another bar on top and push together. Fill the remaining cookies this way.

5 For the topping, melt the milk chocolate and the remaining butter. Drizzle the chocolate over the top of the cookies, then leave to set.

Nutritional information per cookie: Energy 189kcal/790kJ; Protein 2.4g; Carbohydrate 18.8g, of which sugars 11g; Fat 12.1g, of which saturates 7.5g; Cholesterol 22mg; Calcium 50mg; Fibre 0.6g; Sodium 88mg.

Cookies for entertaining

It is always good to have a plate of freshly

baked cookies on stand-by for guests,

who are sure to be delighted when offered

a cookie from this superb collection.

The mouthwatering treats range from

Tiramisu Cookies to Praline Pavlova

Cookies and even Midnight Cookies that

cook overnight while you sleep – perfect

for weekend visitors.

Praline pavlova cookies

Crisp, melt-in-the-mouth meringue with a luxurious velvety chocolate filling is topped with nutty praline – just the thing for a special tea party or simply when you feel in need of a treat.

MAKES 14

2 large (US extra large) egg whites
large pinch of ground cinnamon
90g/3¹/₂oz/¹/₂ cup caster
 (superfine) sugar
50g/2oz/¹/₂ cup pecans, finely chopped

FOR THE FILLING
50g/2oz/¹/₄ cup unsalted (sweet) butter,
 at room temperature, diced

100g/3³/₄oz/scant 1 cup icing
 (confectioners') sugar, sifted
50g/2oz plain (semisweet) chocolate

FOR THE PRALINE
60ml/4 tbsp caster
 (superfine) sugar
15g/¹/₂oz/1 tbsp finely chopped
 toasted almonds

1 Preheat the oven to 140°C/275°F/Gas 1. Line two baking sheets with baking parchment. Put the egg whites in a bowl and whisk until stiff. Stir the cinnamon into the sugar. Add a spoonful of sugar to the egg whites and whisk well. Continue adding the sugar, a spoonful at a time, whisking well until the mixture is thick and glossy. Stir in the chopped pecan nuts.

2 Place 14 spoonfuls of meringue on the prepared baking sheets, spaced well apart. Using the back of a wetted teaspoon, make a small hollow in the top of each meringue. Bake in the oven for 45–60 minutes until dry and just beginning to colour. Remove from the oven and set aside to cool.

3 For the filling, beat together the butter and icing sugar until light and creamy. Break the chocolate into even pieces and place in a heatproof bowl. Set over a pan of barely simmering water and stir occasionally until melted. Leave to cool slightly. Add the chocolate to the butter mixture and stir well. Divide the filling among the meringues, putting a little in each hollow.

4 For the praline, put the sugar in a non-stick frying pan. Heat gently until the sugar melts to form a clear liquid. When the mixture begins to turn brown, stir in the nuts. When the mixture is a golden brown, remove from the heat and pour immediately on to a lightly oiled or non-stick baking sheet. Leave to cool completely and then break into small pieces. Sprinkle over the meringues and serve.

Nutritional information per cookie: Energy 148kcal/621kJ; Protein 1.3g; Carbohydrate 21.2g, of which sugars 21.1g; Fat 7g, of which saturates 2.7g; Cholesterol 8mg; Calcium 16mg; Fibre 0.3g; Sodium 32mg.

Tiramisu cookies

These delicate cookies taste like the wonderful Italian dessert with its flavours of coffee, chocolate, rum and rich creamy custard. Serve with coffee or cups of frothy hot chocolate.

MAKES 14

50g/2oz/¼ cup butter, at room
    temperature, diced
90g/3½oz/½ cup caster
    (superfine) sugar
1 egg, beaten
50g/2oz/½ cup plain (all-purpose) flour

FOR THE FILLING

15ml/1 tbsp dark rum
2.5ml/½ tsp instant coffee powder
15ml/1 tbsp light muscovado
    (brown) sugar
150g/5oz/²⁄₃ cup mascarpone cheese

FOR THE TOPPING

75g/3oz white chocolate
15ml/1 tbsp milk
30ml/2 tbsp crushed chocolate flakes

1 For the filling, mix the rum and coffee powder, stirring until the coffee has dissolved. Put the rum and coffee mixture and the sugar with the mascarpone cheese in a bowl and mix. Cover with clear film (plastic wrap) and chill. Preheat the oven to 200°C/400°F/Gas 6. Line two baking sheets with baking parchment.

2 To make the cookies, cream together the butter and sugar until light and fluffy. Add the egg and mix well. Stir in the flour and mix until combined. Put the mixture into a piping (pastry) bag fitted with a 1cm/½in plain nozzle and pipe 28 small blobs on to the baking sheets. Cook for about 6–8 minutes until firm in the centre. Remove from the oven and allow to cool.

3 To assemble, spread the filling on to half the cookies and place the other halves on top. Melt the chocolate and milk in a heatproof bowl over a pan of hot water. When it has melted, stir to a smooth spreadable consistency. Spread the topping over the cookies, then sprinkle with chocolate flakes.

Nutritional information per cookie: Energy 124kcal/519kJ; Protein 2.3g; Carbohydrate 14.1g, of which sugars 11.4g; Fat 6.6g, of which saturates 4g; Cholesterol 26mg; Calcium 27mg; Fibre 0.1g; Sodium 34mg.

Chocolate and prune cookies

When freshly baked, these cookies have a deliciously gooey centre. As they cool down the mixture hardens to form a firmer, fudge-like consistency. Try these with a glass of brandy.

MAKES 18

150g/5oz/²/₃ cup butter, at room
    temperature, diced
150g/5oz/³/₄ cup caster
    (superfine) sugar
1 egg yolk
250g/9oz/2¹/₄ cups self-raising
    (self-rising) flour
25g/1oz/¹/₄ cup unsweetened
    cocoa powder
about 90g/3¹/₂oz plain (semisweet)
    chocolate, coarsely chopped

FOR THE TOPPING
50g/2oz plain (semisweet)
    chocolate, melted
9 ready-to-eat prunes, halved

1 Preheat the oven to 190°C/375°F/Gas 5. Line two baking sheets with baking parchment. Cream the butter and sugar together until creamy. Beat in the egg yolk. Sift over the flour and cocoa and stir in to make a firm dough.

2 Roll out about a third of the dough on baking parchment. Using a 5cm/2in round biscuit (cookie) cutter, stamp out 18 rounds and place them on the baking sheets. Sprinkle the chopped chocolate in the centre of each cookie.

3 Roll out the remaining dough and, using a 7.5cm/3in round biscuit cutter, stamp out 18 "lids". Lay the lids over the cookie bases and press the edges together. Bake for 10 minutes until just firm to a touch. Leave for 5 minutes, then transfer to a wire rack to cool completely.

4 Dip the cut side of the prunes in the melted chocolate then place one on top of each cookie. Spoon any remaining chocolate over the prunes.

Nutritional information per cookie: Energy 197kcal/825kJ; Protein 2.3g; Carbohydrate 26.4g, of which sugars 15.5g; Fat 9.8g, of which saturates 5.9g; Cholesterol 29mg; Calcium 33mg; Fibre 1.1g; Sodium 66mg.

Lace cookies

Very pretty, delicate and crisp, these lacy cookies are perfect for serving with elegant creamy or iced desserts at the end of a dinner party. Don't be tempted to bake more than four on a sheet.

MAKES ABOUT 14

75g/3oz/6 tbsp butter, diced
75g/3oz/3/4 cup rolled oats
115g/4oz/generous 1/2 cup golden
   caster (superfine) sugar
1 egg, beaten
10ml/2 tsp plain
   (all-purpose) flour
5ml/1 tsp baking powder
2.5ml/1/2 tsp mixed
   (apple pie) spice

1 Preheat the oven to 180°C/350°F/Gas 4. Line three or four large baking sheets with baking parchment.

2 Put the butter in a small heavy pan and set over a low heat until just melted. Remove the pan from the heat. Stir the rolled oats into the melted butter. Add the remaining ingredients and mix well.

3 Place 3 or 4 heaped teaspoonfuls of the mixture, spaced well apart, on each of the baking sheets.

4 Bake for 5–7 minutes, or until golden brown all over. Leave on the baking sheets for a few minutes. Carefully cut the parchment so you can lift each cookie singly. Invert on to a wire rack and remove the parchment. Leave to cool.

Nutritional information per cookie: Energy 101kcal/425kJ; Protein 1.3g; Carbohydrate 13.1g, of which sugars 8.6g; Fat 5.3g, of which saturates 2.9g; Cholesterol 25mg; Calcium 11mg; Fibre 0.4g; Sodium 40mg.

Florentine bites

Very sweet and rich, these little mouthfuls are ideal with after-dinner coffee and liqueurs, and would also make a special gift to offer to a dinner party host.

MAKES 36

200g/7oz good quality plain (semisweet) chocolate (minimum 70 per cent cocoa solids)
50g/2oz/2¹/₂ cups cornflakes
50g/2oz/scant ¹/₂ cup sultanas (golden raisins)
115g/4oz/1 cup toasted flaked (sliced) almonds
115g/4oz/¹/₂ cup glacé (candied) cherries, halved
50g/2oz/¹/₃ cup cut mixed (candied) peel
200ml/7fl oz/scant 1 cup sweetened condensed milk

1 Preheat the oven to 180°C/350°F/Gas 4. Line the base of a shallow 20cm/8in square cake tin (pan) with baking parchment. Lightly grease the sides.

2 Melt the chocolate in a heatproof bowl set over a pan of hot water. Spread the melted chocolate evenly over the base of the tin. Put in the refrigerator to set.

3 Meanwhile, put the cornflakes, sultanas, almonds, cherries and mixed peel in a large bowl. Pour over the condensed milk and toss the mixture gently, using a fork.

4 Spread the mixture evenly over the chocolate base and bake for 12–15 minutes until golden brown. Cool in the tin, then chill for 20 minutes. Cut into tiny squares.

Nutritional information per cookie: Energy 87kcal/364kJ; Protein 1.6g; Carbohydrate 12g, of which sugars 10.7g; Fat 3.9g, of which saturates 1.4g; Cholesterol 2mg; Calcium 30mg; Fibre 0.5g; Sodium 27mg.

Sablés with caramel glaze

These are very buttery French cookies with a dark caramel glaze. The leftover glaze can be kept in the refrigerator and used to flavour fruit salads and especially oranges, both of which are good served with sablés. Use on the day of baking for the most delicious results.

MAKES ABOUT 18

200g/7oz/1³⁄₄ cups plain
  (all-purpose) flour
pinch of salt
75g/3oz/²⁄₃ cup icing
  (confectioners') sugar
130g/4¹⁄₂oz/generous ¹⁄₂ cup unsalted
  (sweet) butter, chilled and diced
3 egg yolks

2.5ml/¹⁄₂ tsp vanilla extract
1 egg yolk, for glazing

FOR THE CARAMEL SYRUP

50g/2oz/¹⁄₄ cup granulated sugar
20ml/4 tsp water
2.5ml/¹⁄₂ tsp lemon juice
50ml/2fl oz/¹⁄₄ cup water

1 First make the caramel syrup. Put the sugar, 20ml/4 tsp water and lemon juice into a small pan. Place over a gentle heat and stir until no longer cloudy. Boil until bubbly and allow to become a rich golden brown. Once this colour, remove from the heat and plunge the base of the pan into a bowl of cold water to stop the cooking. Carefully stir in the 50ml/2fl oz/¹⁄₄ cup water. Set aside to cool completely.

2 Preheat the oven to 180°C/350°F/Gas 4. Put all the cookie ingredients, except the egg yolks and vanilla, into a food processor and process until the mixture resembles breadcrumbs. Add the egg yolks and vanilla and blend until the mixture begins to come together as a firm dough. Wrap in clear film (plastic wrap) and chill for 15 minutes.

3 Roll the dough out on baking parchment to a thickness of 5mm/¹⁄₄in. Using a 7.5cm/3in fluted biscuit (cookie) cutter, stamp out rounds and place them on non-stick baking sheets.

4 Beat the egg yolk with 15ml/1 tbsp of the caramel glaze in a small bowl, then brush sparingly over the cookies. Leave to dry then apply a second thin layer. Using a fork, prick the cookies, then mark in a neat checked pattern by dragging the tines of the fork over the glaze. Bake for about 10–15 minutes, or until crisp and golden brown. Transfer to a wire rack to cool.

Nutritional information per cookie: Energy 129kcal/541kJ; Protein 1.6g; Carbohydrate 15.9g, of which sugars 7.5g; Fat 7g, of which saturates 4g; Cholesterol 49mg; Calcium 24mg; Fibre 0.3g; Sodium 46mg.

Apple crumble and custard slice

These luscious apple slices are easy to make using ready-made sweet pastry and custard. Just think, all the ingredients of one of the world's most popular puddings – in a cookie.

MAKES 16

350g/12oz ready-made sweet pastry
1 large cooking apple, about 250g/9oz
30ml/2 tbsp caster (superfine) sugar
60ml/4 tbsp ready-made thick custard

FOR THE CRUMBLE TOPPING
115g/4oz/1 cup plain (all-purpose) flour
2.5ml/¹/₂ tsp ground cinnamon
60ml/4 tbsp granulated sugar
90g/3¹/₂oz/7 tbsp unsalted (sweet)
   butter, melted

1 Preheat the oven to 190°C/375°F/Gas 5. Roll out the pastry and use to line the base of a 28 x 18cm/11 x 7in shallow cake tin (pan). Prick the pastry with a fork, line with foil and baking beans and bake blind for 10–15 minutes. Remove the foil and baking beans and return the pastry to the oven for a further 5 minutes until cooked and golden brown.

2 Meanwhile, peel, core and chop the apple evenly. Place in a pan with the sugar. Heat gently until the sugar dissolves. Cover and cook for 5–7 minutes until a thick purée is formed. Beat with a wooden spoon and leave to cool.

3 Mix the cold apple with the custard. Spread over the pastry.

4 To make the crumble topping, put the flour, cinnamon and sugar into a bowl and pour over the melted butter. Stir until the mixture forms small clumps. Sprinkle the crumble over the filling. Return to the oven and bake for about 10–15 minutes until the crumble topping is cooked and golden brown. Leave to cool in the tin, then slice into bars to serve.

Nutritional information per cookie: Energy 196kcal/822kJ; Protein 2.1g; Carbohydrate 23.7g, of which sugars 8.1g; Fat 11g, of which saturates 4.9g; Cholesterol 15mg; Calcium 37mg; Fibre 0.9g; Sodium 124mg.

Creamy fig and peach squares

A sweet cream cheese and dried fruit filling with a hint of mint makes these cookies really special. They are ideal for quietening hunger pangs after school or work.

MAKES 24

350g/12oz/3 cups plain
  (all-purpose) flour
200g/7oz/scant 1 cup unsalted
  (sweet) butter, diced
1 egg, beaten
caster (superfine) sugar,
  for sprinkling

FOR THE FILLING

500g/1¼lb/2½ cups ricotta cheese
115g/4oz/generous ½ cup
  caster (superfine) sugar
5ml/1 tsp finely chopped fresh mint
50g/2oz/⅓ cup ready-to-eat dried
  figs, chopped
50g/2oz/⅓ cup ready-to-eat dried
  peaches, chopped

1 Preheat the oven to 190°C/375°F/Gas 5. And then lightly grease a 33 x 23cm/13 x 9in Swiss roll tin (jelly roll pan) or shallow cake tin (pan). Put the flour and butter into a bowl. Rub in the butter until the mixture resembles fine breadcrumbs. Add the egg and enough water to mix to a firm but not sticky dough.

2 Divide the pastry into two and roll out one piece to fit the base of the prepared tin. Place in the tin and trim.

3 To make the filling, put all the ingredients in a bowl and mix together. Spread over the pastry base. Roll out the remaining pastry and place on top of the filling. Prick lightly all over with a fork then sprinkle with caster sugar.

4 Bake for about 30 minutes until light golden brown. Remove from the oven and sprinkle more caster sugar thickly over the top. Cool and cut into slices to serve.

Nutritional information per cookie: Energy 179kcal/747kJ; Protein 3.8g; Carbohydrate 18.8g, of which sugars 7.7g; Fat 10.3g, of which saturates 6.3g; Cholesterol 34mg; Calcium 32mg; Fibre 0.7g; Sodium 56mg.

Candied peel crumble cookies

Crumbly, melt-in-the-mouth cookies, these incorporate candied peel, walnuts and white chocolate chips and are coated with a zingy lemon glaze.

MAKES ABOUT 24

175g/6oz/³⁄4 cup unsalted (sweet)
   butter, at room temperature, diced
90g/3¹⁄2oz/¹⁄2 cup caster
   (superfine) sugar
1 egg, beaten
finely grated rind of 1 lemon
200g/7oz/1³⁄4 cups self-raising
   (self-rising) flour
90g/3¹⁄2oz/generous ¹⁄2 cup
   candied peel, chopped

75g/3oz/³⁄4 cup chopped walnuts
50g/2oz/¹⁄3 cup white chocolate chips

FOR THE GLAZE
50g/2oz/¹⁄2 cup icing (confectioners')
   sugar, sifted
15ml/1 tbsp lemon juice
thin strips of candied peel, to
   decorate (optional)

1 Preheat the oven to 180°C/350°F/Gas 4. Grease two baking sheets or line them with baking parchment.

2 Put the butter and sugar in a large bowl and cream together. Add the egg and beat thoroughly. Add the lemon rind and flour and stir together gently. Finally, fold the candied peel, walnuts and chocolate chips into the mixture.

3 Place tablespoonfuls of mixture, spaced slightly apart, on the baking sheets and bake for 12–15 minutes, until cooked but still pale in colour. Transfer the cookies to a wire rack.

4 For the glaze, put the icing sugar in a bowl and stir in the lemon juice. Spoon glaze over each cookie. Decorate with candied peel, if using.

Nutritional information per cookie: Energy 150kcal/626kJ; Protein 1.8g; Carbohydrate 16.2g, of which sugars 9.8g; Fat 9.2g, of which saturates 4.4g; Cholesterol 23mg; Calcium 31mg; Fibre 0.5g; Sodium 61mg.

Mini fudge bites

These cute little cookies have the flavour of butterscotch and fudge and are topped with chopped pecan nuts for a delicious crunch – just the right size for a special little treat.

MAKES ABOUT 40

200g/7oz/1³/₄ cups self-raising (self-rising) flour
115g/4oz/¹/₂ cup butter, at room temperature, diced
115g/4oz/generous ¹/₂ cup dark muscovado (molasses) sugar
75g/3oz vanilla cream fudge, diced
1 egg, beaten
25g/1oz/¹/₄ cup pecan nut halves, sliced widthways

1 Preheat the oven to 190°C/375°F/Gas 5. Then line two or three large baking sheets with baking parchment.

2 Put the flour in a bowl and rub in the butter until the mixture resembles fine breadcrumbs. Add the muscovado sugar and diced vanilla cream fudge to the flour mixture and stir together well until combined.

3 Add the beaten egg and mix in well. Bring the dough together with your hands, then knead on a floured surface. It will be soft yet firm.

4 Roll the dough into two equal cylinders, 23cm/9in long. Cut into 1cm/¹/₂in slices and place on the baking sheets. Sprinkle over the nuts and press in lightly. Bake for 12 minutes until browned at the edges. Transfer to a wire rack to cool.

Nutritional information per cookie: Energy 65kcal/269kJ; Protein 0.8g; Carbohydrate 8.5g, of which sugars 4.7g; Fat 3.3g, of which saturates 1.7g; Cholesterol 11.3mg; Calcium 12.8mg; Fibre 0.2g; Sodium 22mg.

Midnight cookies

These cookies are so called because you can make them up before you go to bed and leave them to bake slowly in the switched-off oven. Hey presto – there they are in the morning.

MAKES 9

1 egg white
90g/3¹/₂oz/¹/₂ cup caster
  (superfine) sugar
50g/2oz/¹/₂ cup ground almonds
90g/3¹/₂oz/generous ¹/₂ cup milk
  chocolate chips
90g/3¹/₂oz/scant ¹/₂ cup glacé
  (candied) cherries, chopped
50g/2oz/²/₃ cup sweetened,
  shredded coconut

1 Preheat the oven to 220°C/425°F/Gas 7. Line a large baking sheet with baking parchment.

2 Put the egg white in a large, clean, grease-free bowl and whisk until stiff peaks form. Add the caster sugar, a spoonful at a time, whisking well between each addition until all of the sugar is fully incorporated.

3 When the mixture is completely smooth and glossy in appearance, fold in the almonds, chocolate chips, cherries and coconut. Carefully place 9 spoonfuls on the baking sheet, making sure they are well spaced out.

4 Place in the oven, close the door then turn the oven off. Leave overnight (or at least 6 hours) and don't open the door. Serve the cookies for breakfast.

Nutritional information per cookie: Energy 185kcal/777kJ; Protein 2.7g; Carbohydrate 23.5g, of which sugars 23.4g; Fat 9.6g, of which saturates 5g; Cholesterol 2mg; Calcium 48mg; Fibre 1.3g; Sodium 21mg.

Tea finger cookies

The unusual ingredient in these cookies is Lady Grey tea – similar to Earl Grey but with the addition of Seville orange and lemon peel – which imparts a subtle flavour.

MAKES ABOUT 36

150g/5oz/10 tbsp unsalted (sweet)
   butter, at room temperature, diced
115g/4oz/generous ½ cup light
   muscovado (brown) sugar
15–30ml/1–2 tbsp Lady Grey tea leaves

1 egg, beaten
200g/7oz/1¾ cups plain
   (all-purpose) flour
demerara (raw) sugar, for sprinkling

1 Preheat the oven to 190°C/375°F/Gas 5. Line two or three baking sheets with baking parchment.

2 Beat the butter and sugar until light and creamy. Stir in the Lady Grey tea leaves until well combined. Beat in the egg, then carefully fold in the flour.

3 Using your hands, roll the dough on a lightly floured surface into a long cylinder, about 23cm/9in long. Press down on the top of the dough cylinder with the palm of your hand to flatten slightly.

4 Wrap the dough in clear film (plastic wrap) and chill for about 1 hour until the dough is firm enough to slice.

5 Using a sharp knife, cut the dough cylinder widthways into 5mm/¼in slices and place, slightly apart, on the prepared baking sheets. Sprinkle the cookies with a little demerara sugar.

6 Bake for 10–15 minutes until lightly browned. Using a metal spatula, transfer the cookies to a wire rack and leave to cool completely before serving.

Nutritional information per cookie: Energy 65kcal/270kJ; Protein 0.7g; Carbohydrate 7.7g, of which sugars 3.4g; Fat 3.7g, of which saturates 2.2g; Cholesterol 14mg; Calcium 11mg; Fibre 0.2g; Sodium 28mg.

Almond and vanilla cookies
with praline coating

These short-textured almond cookies, filled with vanilla cream and coated in praline, are just the thing to have with an espresso – a sweet bonne bouche to counter the strong coffee.

MAKES 17–18

150g/5oz/1¼ cups plain
   (all-purpose) flour
75g/3oz/¾ cup ground almonds
75g/3oz/6 tbsp unsalted
   (sweet) butter, at room
   temperature, diced
1 egg yolk
5ml/1 tsp vanilla extract
icing (confectioners') sugar, sifted,
   for dusting

FOR THE PRALINE
25g/1oz/¼ cup whole blanched almonds
50g/2oz/¼ cup caster (superfine) sugar

FOR THE FILLING
150g/5oz/1¼ cups icing
   (confectioners') sugar, sifted
75g/3oz/6 tbsp unsalted (sweet) butter,
   at room temperature, diced
5ml/1 tsp vanilla extract

1 First make the praline. Lightly oil a baking sheet and place the almonds on it, fairly close together. Melt the sugar in a small non-stick pan over a low heat. Continue heating until it turns dark golden brown and pour over the almonds. Set aside to cool. Crush the praline finely in a food processor.

2 Preheat the oven to 160°C/325°F/Gas 3. Line three baking sheets with baking parchment. Put the flour, ground almonds and butter in a bowl. Rub together until the mixture starts to cling together. Add the egg yolk and vanilla and work together to make a soft but not sticky dough.

3 Roll out to a thickness of 5mm/¼in on baking parchment. Using a 5cm/2in round cutter, stamp out rounds and place them on the baking sheets. Bake for 15–20 minutes until golden brown. Leave for 5 minutes, then cool on a wire rack.

4 For the filling, beat together the icing sugar, butter and vanilla until creamy, then use to sandwich the cookies in pairs. Press the cookies so the filling oozes out of the sides and smooth around the sides of the cookie. Put the praline on a plate and roll the edges of each cookie in the praline until thickly coated. Dust the tops of the cookies with icing sugar.

Nutritional information per cookie: Energy 172kcal/717kJ; Protein 2.2g; Carbohydrate 18.5g, of which sugars 12g; Fat 10.4g, of which saturates 4.7g; Cholesterol 29mg; Calcium 34mg; Fibre 0.7g; Sodium 53mg.

Rosemary-scented citrus tuiles

These delicious crisp cookies are flavoured with tangy orange and lemon rind, and made beautifully fragrant with fresh rosemary – an unusual but winning combination.

MAKES 18–20

50g/2oz/¼ cup unsalted (sweet) butter, diced

2 egg whites

115g/4oz/generous ½ cup caster (superfine) sugar

finely grated rind of ½ lemon

finely grated rind of ½ orange

10ml/2 tsp finely chopped fresh rosemary

50g/2oz/½ cup plain (all-purpose) flour

1 Preheat the oven to 190°C/ 375°F/Gas 5. Line a baking sheet with baking parchment. Melt the butter in a pan over a low heat. Leave to cool. Whisk the egg whites until stiff, then whisk in the sugar.

2 Fold in the lemon and orange rinds, rosemary and flour and then the melted butter. Place 2 large tablespoonfuls of mixture on the baking sheet.

3 Spread each spoonful of the mixture to a thin disc about 9cm/3½in in diameter. Bake for about 5–6 minutes until golden.

4 Remove from the oven and lift the tuiles using a metal spatula and drape over a rolling pin. Transfer to a wire rack when set in a curved shape. Continue baking the rest of the mixture in the same way.

Nutritional information per cookie: Energy 51kcal/214kJ; Protein 0.6g; Carbohydrate 8g, of which sugars 6.1g; Fat 2.1g, of which saturates 1.3g; Cholesterol 5mg; Calcium 7mg; Fibre 0.1g; Sodium 22mg.

Ginger glass cookies

As thin, delicate and elegant as fine glass, these ginger cookies are ideal served with creamy desserts, syllabubs, sorbets and luxury ice creams.

MAKES ABOUT 18

50g/2oz/1/4 cup unsalted (sweet)
   butter, diced
40g/11/2oz/3 tbsp liquid glucose
   (clear corn syrup)
90g/31/2oz/1/2 cup caster
   (superfine) sugar
40g/11/2oz/1/3 cup plain
   (all-purpose) flour
5ml/1 tsp ground ginger

1 Put the butter and liquid glucose in a heatproof bowl set over a pan of gently simmering water. Stir together until melted. Set aside.

2 Put the sugar in a large bowl and sift over the flour and ginger. Stir into the butter mixture, then beat well until combined. Cover with clear film (plastic wrap) and chill for about 25 minutes, until firm. Meanwhile, preheat the oven to 180°C/350°F/Gas 4 and line three large baking sheets with baking parchment.

3 Roll teaspoonfuls of the mixture into balls and place them, spaced well apart to allow room for spreading, on the baking sheets. Place a second piece of baking parchment on top and roll the cookies thinly. Peel off the top sheet. Stamp each cookie with a 7.5 or 9cm/3 or 31/2in plain round cutter.

4 Bake for 5–6 minutes, or until golden. Leave for a few seconds on the baking sheets, then either leave flat or curl over in half. Allow to cool completely.

Nutritional information per cookie: Energy 55kcal/231kJ; Protein 0.3g; Carbohydrate 8.9g, of which sugars 6.2g; Fat 2.3g, of which saturates 1.5g; Cholesterol 6mg; Calcium 6mg; Fibre 0.1g; Sodium 21mg.

Chocolate and pistachio wedges

These cookies are rich and grainy textured, with a bitter chocolate flavour. They go extremely well with vanilla ice cream and are especially delicious with bananas and custard.

MAKES 16

200g/7oz/scant 1 cup unsalted (sweet)
  butter, at room temperature, diced
90g/3¹/₂oz/¹/₂ cup golden caster
  (superfine) sugar
250g/9oz/2¹/₄ cups plain
  (all-purpose) flour
50g/2oz/¹/₂ cup unsweetened
  cocoa powder
25g/1oz/¹/₄ cup shelled pistachio nuts,
  finely chopped
unsweetened cocoa powder, for dusting

1 Preheat the oven to 180°C/350°F/Gas 4 and line a shallow 23cm/9in round sandwich tin (pan) with baking parchment.

2 Beat the butter and sugar until light and creamy. Sift the flour and cocoa powder, then add the flour mixture to the butter and work in with your hands until the mixture is smooth.

3 Gently knead the mixture until it is soft and pliable then press into the prepared round sandwich tin.

4 Using the back of a tablespoon, spread the mixture evenly in the tin. Sprinkle the pistachios over the top and press in gently. Prick with a fork, then mark into 16 segments using a round-bladed knife.

5 Bake for 15–20 minutes in the oven. Do not allow them to brown at all or the cookies will taste bitter. Remove from the oven and dust the cookies with cocoa. Cut through the marked sections with a round-bladed knife and cool.

Nutritional information per cookie: Energy 188kcal/783kJ; Protein 2.4g; Carbohydrate 18.6g, of which sugars 6.3g; Fat 12g, of which saturates 7.1g; Cholesterol 27mg; Calcium 33mg; Fibre 1g; Sodium 115mg.

Chocolate truffle cookies

Deeply decadent, chocolatey truffle cookies are given a wicked twist by the addition of cherry brandy – the perfect way to end dinner.

MAKES 18

50g/2oz/$\frac{1}{2}$ cup plain
  (all-purpose) flour
25g/1oz/$\frac{1}{4}$ cup unsweetened
  cocoa powder
2.5ml/$\frac{1}{2}$ tsp baking powder
90g/3$\frac{1}{2}$oz/$\frac{1}{2}$ cup caster
  (superfine) sugar
25g/1oz/2 tbsp butter, diced
1 egg, beaten
5ml/1 tsp cherry brandy or fresh
  orange juice
50g/2oz/$\frac{1}{2}$ cup icing
  (confectioners') sugar

1 Preheat the oven to 200°C/400°F/Gas 6. Line two baking sheets with baking parchment. Sift the flour, cocoa and baking powder into a large bowl and stir in the sugar. Rub in the butter until the mixture resembles breadcrumbs.

2 Mix together the beaten egg and cherry brandy or orange juice and stir into the flour mixture. Cover and chill for 30 minutes.

3 Put the icing sugar into a bowl. Shape walnut-size pieces of dough roughly into a ball and drop into the icing sugar. Toss until thickly coated then place on to the prepared baking sheets.

4 Bake the cookies for about 10 minutes, or until just set.

5 Using a metal spatula, transfer the cookies to a wire rack and allow to cool completely before serving.

Nutritional information per cookie: Energy 59kcal/249kJ; Protein 0.9g; Carbohydrate 10.5g, of which sugars 8.2g; Fat 1.8g, of which saturates 1g; Cholesterol 14mg; Calcium 12mg; Fibre 0.3g; Sodium 26mg.

Brownies, bars and no-bake cookies

Brownies and bars make filling snacks, and perfect picnic fare. There are probably more variations on the brownie than on any other cookie. As for bars, almost anything's possible – crisp, nutty, chewy or succulent. No-bake cookies couldn't be easier to make and are a great way for children to get involved in the kitchen.

Butterscotch brownies

These gorgeous treats are made with brown sugar, white chocolate chips and walnuts. Who could possibly have the willpower to resist? You might want to make two batches at a time.

MAKES 12

450g/1lb white chocolate chips
75g/3oz/6 tbsp unsalted (sweet) butter
3 eggs
175g/6oz/¾ cup light muscovado (brown) sugar
175g/6oz/1½ cups self-raising (self-rising) flour
175g/6oz/1½ cups walnuts, chopped
5ml/1 tsp vanilla extract

1 Preheat the oven to 190°C/ 375°F/Gas 5. Line the base of a 28 x 18cm/11 x 7in shallow tin (pan) with baking parchment. Lightly grease the sides.

2 Melt 90g/3½oz of the chocolate chips with the butter in a bowl set over a pan of hot water. Leave to cool slightly.

3 Put the eggs and light muscovado sugar into a large bowl and whisk well, then whisk in the melted chocolate mixture.

4 Sift the flour into the bowl and gently fold in along with the chopped walnuts, vanilla extract and the remaining chocolate chips. Be careful not to overmix.

5 Spread the mixture out in the tin and bake for 30 minutes, or until risen and golden brown. The centre should be firm to the touch but will be slightly soft until it cools down.

6 Leave to cool in the tin, then cut into 12 bars when the brownie is completely cool.

Nutritional information per cookie: Energy 469kcal/1961kJ; Protein 8.1g; Carbohydrate 48.7g, of which sugars 37.7g; Fat 28.3g, of which saturates 11.4g; Cholesterol 61mg; Calcium 182mg; Fibre 1g; Sodium 151mg.

White chocolate brownies

These irresistible brownies are packed full of creamy white chocolate and lots of juicy dried fruit.
They are best served cut into very small bitesize portions as they are incredibly rich.

MAKES 18

75g/3oz/6 tbsp unsalted (sweet)
    butter, diced
400g/14oz white chocolate, chopped
3 eggs
90g/3¹/₂oz/¹/₂ cup golden caster
    (superfine) sugar
10ml/2 tsp vanilla extract
90g/3¹/₂oz/³/₄ cup sultanas
    (golden raisins)
coarsely grated rind of 1 lemon, plus
    15ml/1 tbsp juice
200g/7oz/1³/₄ cups plain
    (all-purpose) flour

1 Preheat the oven to 190°C/ 375°F/ Gas 5. Grease and line a 28 x 20cm/11 x 8in shallow baking tin (pan) with baking parchment.

2 Put the butter and 300g/11oz of the chocolate in a bowl and melt over a pan of simmering water.

3 Remove from the heat and beat in the eggs and sugar. Add the vanilla, sultanas, lemon rind and juice, flour and the remaining chocolate.

4 Tip the mixture into the prepared tin and spread the mixture right into the corners.

5 Bake for about 20 minutes, or until slightly risen and the surface is only just turning golden. The centre should still be slightly soft.

6 Leave to cool in the tin. Using a sharp knife, cut the brownies into small squares and remove from the tin before serving.

Nutritional information per cookie: Energy 232kcal/973kJ; Protein 4g; Carbohydrate 30.3g, of which sugars 21.8g; Fat 11.4g, of which saturates 6.5g; Cholesterol 41mg; Calcium 86mg; Fibre 0.4g; Sodium 65mg.

Chocolate cheesecake brownies

A very dense chocolate brownie mixture is swirled with creamy cheese to give a marbled effect. Cut into tiny squares for little mouthfuls of absolute heaven.

MAKES 16

FOR THE CHEESECAKE MIXTURE
1 egg
225g/8oz/1 cup full-fat cream cheese
50g/2oz/¼ cup caster (superfine) sugar
5ml/1 tsp vanilla extract

FOR THE BROWNIE MIXTURE
115g/4oz dark (bittersweet)
  chocolate (minimum 70 per cent
  cocoa solids)
115g/4oz/½ cup unsalted
  (sweet) butter
150g/5oz/¾ cup light muscovado
  (brown) sugar
2 eggs, beaten
50g/2oz/½ cup plain (all-purpose) flour

1 Preheat the oven to 160°C/325°F/Gas 3. Line the base and sides of a 20cm/8in cake tin (pan) with baking parchment.

2 For the cheesecake mixture, beat the egg in a bowl, then add the cream cheese, caster sugar and vanilla. Beat together until smooth and creamy.

3 For the brownie mixture, melt the chocolate and butter in a heatproof bowl set over a pan of simmering water. Remove from the heat, stir, then add the sugar. Add the eggs, a little at a time, and beat well. Stir in the flour.

4 Spread two-thirds of the brownie mixture over the base of the tin. Spread the cheesecake mixture on top, then spoon on the remaining brownie mixture in heaps. Using a skewer, swirl the mixtures together. Bake for about 30–35 minutes, or until just set in the centre. Leave to cool in the tin, then cut into squares.

Nutritional information per cookie: Energy 226kcal/940kJ; Protein 2.4g; Carbohydrate 20.1g, of which sugars 17.7g; Fat 15.7g, of which saturates 9.4g; Cholesterol 65mg; Calcium 34mg; Fibre 0.3g; Sodium 100mg.

Fudge-nut bars

You can use any kind of nut for these fudgy treats, from mild-flavoured almonds, peanuts or macadamia nuts to slightly stronger pecans or hazelnuts.

MAKES 16

150g/5oz/10 tbsp unsalted (sweet)
   butter, chilled and diced
250g/9oz/2¹/₄ cups plain
   (all-purpose) flour
75g/3oz/scant ¹/₂ cup caster
   (superfine) sugar

FOR THE TOPPING

150g/5oz milk chocolate, broken
   into pieces
40g/1¹/₂oz/3 tbsp unsalted butter
405g/14¹/₄oz can sweetened
   condensed milk
50g/2oz/¹/₂ cup chopped nuts

1 Preheat the oven to 160°C/ 325°F/Gas 3. Grease a 28 x 18cm/11 x 7in shallow baking tin (pan).

2 Put the butter and flour in a food processor and process until the mixture resembles breadcrumbs. Add the sugar and process until the mixture starts to cling together. Tip the mixture into the tin and spread out evenly. Bake for 35–40 minutes until the surface is lightly coloured.

3 Put the chocolate in a pan with the butter and condensed milk. Heat gently until the chocolate and butter have melted, then increase the heat and cook, stirring, for 3–5 minutes until the mixture starts to thicken. Add the chopped nuts and pour the mixture evenly over the cookie base. Leave to cool, then chill for at least 2 hours until firm. Serve cut into bars.

Nutritional information per cookie: Energy 315kcal/1317kJ; Protein 4.9g; Carbohydrate 36.6g, of which sugars 24.7g; Fat 17.5g, of which saturates 9.7g; Cholesterol 37mg; Calcium 123mg; Fibre 0.7g; Sodium 116mg.

Luscious lemon bars

A crisp cookie base is covered with a tangy lemon topping. The bars make a delightful addition to the tea table on a warm summer's day in the garden.

MAKES 12

150g/5oz/1¼ cups plain
   (all-purpose) flour
90g/3½oz/7 tbsp unsalted (sweet)
   butter, chilled and diced
50g/2oz/½ cup icing (confectioners')
   sugar, sifted

FOR THE TOPPING
2 eggs
175g/6oz/scant 1 cup caster
   (superfine) sugar
finely grated rind and juice of
   1 large lemon
15ml/1 tbsp plain (all-purpose) flour
2.5ml/½ tsp bicarbonate of soda
   (baking soda)
icing (confectioners') sugar, for dusting

1 Preheat the oven to 180°C/350°F/Gas 4. Line the base of a 20cm/8in square shallow cake tin (pan) with baking parchment and lightly grease the sides of the tin.

2 Process the flour, butter and icing sugar in a food processor until the mixture comes together as a firm dough. Press evenly into the base of the tin and spread smoothly using the back of a tablespoon.

3 Bake for 12–15 minutes until lightly golden. Cool in the tin.

4 To make the topping, whisk the eggs in a bowl until frothy. Add the caster sugar, a little at a time, whisking well between each addition. Whisk in the lemon rind and juice, flour and soda. Pour over the cookie base. Bake for 20–25 minutes, until set and golden.

5 Leave to cool slightly. Cut into 12 bars and dust lightly with icing sugar. Leave to cool completely before serving.

Nutritional information per cookie: Energy 189kcal/795kJ; Protein 2.5g; Carbohydrate 30.3g, of which sugars 19.8g; Fat 7.3g, of which saturates 4.2g; Cholesterol 48mg; Calcium 35mg; Fibre 0.4g; Sodium 59mg.

Sticky treacle slices

This three-layered treat of buttery cookie base, covered with a sticky dried fruit filling, followed by an oaty flapjack-style topping, is utterly delicious and unbelievably easy to make.

MAKES 14

175g/6oz/1¹/₂ cups plain
  (all-purpose) flour
90g/3¹/₂oz/7 tbsp unsalted (sweet)
  butter, diced
50g/2oz/¹/₄ cup caster (superfine) sugar
250g/9oz/generous 1 cup mixed dried
  fruit, such as prunes, apricots, peaches,
  pears and apples, finely chopped
300ml/¹/₂ pint/1¹/₄ cups apple or
  orange juice
225g/8oz/²/₃ cup golden (light
  corn) syrup
finely grated rind of 1 small orange,
  plus 45ml/3 tbsp juice
90g/3¹/₂oz/1 cup rolled oats

1 Preheat the oven to 180°C/350°F/ Gas 4. Grease a 28 x 18cm/11 x 7in baking tin (pan). Put the flour and butter in a food processor and process so it resembles breadcrumbs.

2 Add the sugar and mix. Tip into the tin and press down evenly. Bake for 15 minutes. For the filling, put the dried fruit in a pan with the fruit juice. Bring to the boil, reduce the heat, cover and simmer for 15 minutes until the juice has been absorbed.

3 Leaving the base in the tin, tip the filling over and spread evenly with the back of a spoon.

4 Mix the golden syrup with the orange rind and juice and oats. Spoon over the dried fruits, spreading evenly with the back of a spoon. Return the cookies to the oven for 25 minutes, or until the topping is golden brown. Leave the in the tin to cool completely before cutting into squares to serve.

Nutritional information per cookie: Energy 213kcal/898kJ; Protein 2.6g; Carbohydrate 39.3g, of which sugars 25.1g; Fat 6.1g, of which saturates 3.4g; Cholesterol 14mg; Calcium 35mg; Fibre 1.8g; Sodium 88mg.

Sticky marmalade squares

These baked treats have a plain lower layer supporting a scrumptious nutty upper layer flavoured with orange and chunky marmalade. Cut into squares or bars – whichever you prefer.

MAKES 24

350g/12oz/3 cups plain
   (all-purpose) flour
200g/7oz/scant 1 cup unsalted (sweet)
   butter, diced
150g/5oz/²⁄₃ cup light muscovado
   (molasses) sugar
2.5ml/½ tsp bicarbonate of soda
   (baking soda)
1 egg, beaten
120ml/4fl oz/½ cup single
   (light) cream
50g/2oz/½ cup pecan nuts, chopped
50g/2oz/⅓ cup mixed (candied) peel
90ml/6 tbsp chunky marmalade
   15–30ml/1–2 tbsp orange juice

1 Preheat the oven to 190°C/ 375°F/Gas 5. Line the base of a 28 x 18cm/11 x 7in tin (pan) with baking parchment.

2 Put the flour in a bowl and rub in the butter. Stir in the sugar, then spread half the mixture over the base of the tin. Press down firmly with the back of a spoon.

3 Bake for 10–15 minutes until the cookie base is lightly browned. Leave to cool in the baking tin while the filling is prepared.

4 For the filling, put the remaining flour mixture into a bowl. Stir in the soda. Mix in the egg, cream, pecans, peel and half the marmalade. Pour over the cooled base and bake for 20–25 minutes, or until the filling is just firm and golden brown.

5 Put the remaining marmalade into a small pan and heat gently. Add just enough orange juice to make a spreadable glaze. Brush the glaze over the baked cookie mixture while it is still warm. Leave to cool before cutting into bars or squares.

Nutritional information per cookie: Energy 194kcal/809kJ; Protein 2.1g; Carbohydrate 22g, of which sugars 10.9g; Fat 11.4g, of which saturates 6.2g; Cholesterol 33mg; Calcium 36mg; Fibre 0.7g; Sodium 77mg.

Jewelled shortbread fingers

These delicious fingers are made using a classic, buttery shortbread base, drizzled with icing and decorated with sparkling, crushed sweets and glistening silver balls.

MAKES 14

90g/3¹/₂oz/7 tbsp unsalted (sweet) butter, diced
175g/6oz/1¹/₂ cups plain (all-purpose) flour
50g/2oz/¹/₄ cup caster (superfine) sugar

FOR THE TOPPING
150g/5oz/1¹/₄ cups icing (confectioners') sugar
10–15ml/2–3 tsp lemon juice
coloured boiled sweets (hard candies)
silver balls

1 Preheat the oven to 160°C/325°F/Gas 3. Grease an 18cm/7in square shallow baking tin (pan).

2 Put the butter and flour in a food processor and process until the mixture resembles breadcrumbs. Add the sugar and process until the ingredients cling together. Put the dough in the tin and press down in an even layer. Bake for 35 minutes, or until just beginning to colour. Leave to cool in the tin.

3 For the topping, put the icing sugar in a bowl and add enough lemon juice to make a thick paste that only just holds its shape.

4 Tap the sweets (in their wrappers) gently with a rolling pin to break them into pieces. Unwrap the sweets and mix them together in a bowl. Turn out the shortbread base on to a board. Cut in half, then across into fingers. Drizzle with the icing, then sprinkle with the sweets and silver balls. Leave to set.

Nutritional information per cookie: Energy 147kcal/618kJ; Protein 1.3g; Carbohydrate 24.7g, of which sugars 15.2g; Fat 5.5g, of which saturates 3.4g; Cholesterol 14mg; Calcium 26mg; Fibre 0.4g; Sodium 40mg.

Walnut and honey bars

A sweet, custard-like filling brimming with nuts sits on a crisp pastry base. These scrumptious bars are pure heaven to bite into.

MAKES 12–14

175g/6oz/1½ cups plain
  (all-purpose) flour
30ml/2 tbsp icing (confectioners')
  sugar, sifted
115g/4oz/½ cup unsalted (sweet)
  butter, diced

FOR THE TOPPING

300g/11oz/scant 3 cups walnut halves
2 eggs, beaten
50g/2oz/¼ cup unsalted (sweet)
  butter, melted
50g/2oz/¼ cup light muscovado
  (brown) sugar
90ml/6 tbsp dark clear honey
30ml/2 tbsp single (light) cream

1 Preheat the oven to 190°C/375°F/Gas 5. Lightly grease a 28 x 18cm/ 11 x 7in shallow tin (pan).

2 Put the flour, icing sugar and butter in a food processor and process until the mixture forms crumbs. Using the pulse button, add 15–30ml/1–2 tbsp water – enough to make a firm dough.

3 Roll the dough out on baking parchment and line the base and sides of the tin. Trim and fold the top edge inwards.

4 Prick the base, line with foil and baking beans and bake blind for 10 minutes. Remove the foil and beans. Return the base to the oven for about 5 minutes, until cooked but not browned. Reduce the temperature to 180°C/350°F/Gas 4.

5 For the topping, sprinkle the walnuts over the base. Whisk the remaining ingredients together. Pour over the walnuts and bake for 25 minutes.

Nutritional information per cookie: Energy 333kcal/1386kJ; Protein 5.4g; Carbohydrate 21.4g, of which sugars 11.7g; Fat 25.7g, of which saturates 7.8g; Cholesterol 53mg; Calcium 49mg; Fibre 1.1g; Sodium 85mg.

Rainbow gingerbread squares

These gingerbread squares have a more spongy texture than traditional gingerbread cookies. The ground and preserved stem ginger can be left out for a less-spicy cookie for younger children.

MAKES 16

225g/8oz/2 cups plain
  (all-purpose) flour
5ml/1 tsp baking powder
10ml/2 tsp ground ginger
2 pieces preserved stem ginger from
  a jar, finely chopped
90g/3¹/₂oz/³/₄ cup raisins
50g/2oz/¹/₄ cup glacé (candied)
  cherries, chopped
115g/4oz/¹/₂ cup unsalted (sweet)
  butter, diced
115g/4oz/¹/₃ cup golden (light
  corn) syrup

30ml/2 tbsp black treacle (molasses)
75g/3oz/ ¹/₃ cup dark muscovado
  (molasses) sugar
2 eggs, beaten

FOR THE TOPPING
200g/7oz/1³/₄ cups icing
  (confectioners') sugar
50g/2oz/¹/₄ cup unsalted (sweet)
  butter, at room temperature, diced
multi-coloured sprinkles

1 Preheat the oven to 160°C/325°F/Gas 3. Grease a 20cm/8in square shallow baking or cake tin (pan) and line with baking parchment.

2 Sift the flour, baking powder and ground ginger into a bowl. Add the stem ginger, raisins and cherries and stir well.

3 Put the butter, syrup, treacle and muscovado sugar in a small pan and heat gently until the butter melts. Pour into the dry ingredients. Add the eggs and stir well. Tip the mixture into the tin and spread in an even layer. Bake for 55 minutes, or until risen and firm in the centre. Leave to cool in the tin.

4 For the topping, put the icing sugar and butter in a bowl with 20ml/4 tsp hot water and beat together until smooth and creamy. Turn the gingerbread on to a board. Using a large, sharp knife, carefully cut the gingerbread into 16 squares.

5 Using a teaspoon, drizzle a thick line of icing around the top edge of each gingerbread square. Don't worry if it falls down the sides. Scatter the sprinkles over the icing and leave to set.

Nutritional information per cookie: Energy 251kcal/1057kJ; Protein 2.4g; Carbohydrate 41.9g, of which sugars 31.1g; Fat 9.4g, of which saturates 5.6g; Cholesterol 46mg; Calcium 50mg; Fibre 0.6g; Sodium 100mg.

Almond, orange and carrot bars

An out-of-this-world cookie version of the ever-popular carrot cake, these flavoursome, moist bars are best eaten fresh or stored in the refrigerator after making.

MAKES 16

75g/3oz/6 tbsp unsalted (sweet)
  butter, softened
50g/2oz/¼ cup caster (superfine) sugar
150g/5oz/1¼ cups plain
  (all-purpose) flour
finely grated rind of 1 orange

FOR THE FILLING
90g/3½oz/7 tbsp butter, diced
75g/3oz/½ cup caster (superfine) sugar
2 eggs
2.5ml/½ tsp almond extract
175g/6oz/1½ cups ground almonds
1 cooked carrot, coarsely grated

FOR THE TOPPING
175g/6oz/¾ cup cream cheese
30–45ml/2–3 tbsp chopped walnuts

1 Preheat the oven to 190°C/375°F/Gas 5. Lightly grease a 28 x 18cm/ 11 x 7in shallow baking tin (pan). Put the butter, caster sugar, flour and orange rind into a bowl and rub together until the mixture resembles coarse breadcrumbs. Add water, a teaspoon at a time, to mix to a firm but not sticky dough. Roll out on a lightly floured surface and use to line the base of the tin.

2 To make the filling, cream the butter and sugar together. Beat in the eggs and almond extract. Stir in the ground almonds and the grated carrot. Spread the mixture over the dough base and bake for about 25 minutes until firm in the centre and golden brown. Leave to cool in the tin.

3 To make the topping, beat the cream cheese until smooth and spread it over the cooled, cooked filling. Swirl with a small metal spatula and sprinkle with the chopped walnuts. Cut into bars with a sharp knife and serve.

Nutritional information per cookie: Energy 85kcal/355kJ; Protein 1.4g; Carbohydrate 5.3g, of which sugars 2.9g; Fat 6.6g, of which saturates 3g; Cholesterol 18mg; Calcium 20mg; Fibre 0.4g; Sodium 34mg.

Hazelnut and raspberry bars

The hazelnuts are ground and used to make a superb sweet pastry which is then baked with a layer of raspberry jam in the middle and sprinkled with flaked almonds.

MAKES 30

250g/9oz/2¼ cups hazelnuts
300g/10oz/2½ cups plain
   (all-purpose) flour
5ml/1 tsp mixed (apple pie) spice
2.5ml/½ tsp ground cinnamon
150g/5oz/1¼ cups icing
   (confectioners') sugar
15ml/1 tbsp grated lemon rind
300g/10oz/1¼ cups unsalted (sweet)
   butter, softened
3 egg yolks
350g/12oz/1¼ cups seedless
   raspberry jam

FOR THE TOPPING

1 egg, beaten
15ml/1 tbsp clear honey
50g/2oz/½ cup flaked (sliced) almonds

1 Grind the hazelnuts in a food processor and then put in a bowl. Sift in the flour, spices and icing sugar. Add the lemon rind and mix well, then add the butter and the egg yolks and, using your hands, knead until a smooth dough is formed. Wrap in clear film (plastic wrap) and chill for 30 minutes. Meanwhile, preheat the oven to 200°C/400°F/Gas 6 and lightly grease a 33 x 23cm/13 x 9in Swiss roll tin (jelly roll pan).

2 Roll out half the dough to fit the base of the prepared tin and place in the tin. Spread the jam all over the dough base. Roll out the remaining dough and place on top of the jam.

3 For the topping, beat the egg and honey together and brush over the dough. Sprinkle the almonds evenly over the top. Bake for 10 minutes, then lower the oven temperature to 180°C/350°F/Gas 4 and bake for another 20–30 minutes until golden brown. Cool then cut into bars.

Nutritional information per cookie: Energy 231kcal/962kJ; Protein 2.9g; Carbohydrate 22.1g, of which sugars 14.3g; Fat 15.1g, of which saturates 5.9g; Cholesterol 41mg; Calcium 38mg; Fibre 1g; Sodium 66mg.

Ice mountain

To create an alternative shape to rounds and squares, this unusual refrigerator cookie is allowed to set in the corner of a cake tin, giving it a "pyramid" shape for slicing into triangles.

MAKES 12

75g/3oz malted milk biscuits (cookies)
90g/3¹/₂oz milk chocolate
75g/3oz white chocolate mint sticks
250g/9oz white chocolate

60ml/4 tbsp double (heavy) cream
several clear mints (hard mint candies),
   to decorate

1 Break the biscuits into small pieces, chop the milk chocolate into small dice and break the chocolate mint sticks into short lengths. Keep these ingredients separate.

2 Reserve 50g/2oz of the white chocolate. Break up the remainder and put in a heatproof bowl with the cream. Set the bowl over a pan of simmering water and leave until melted, stirring the chocolate frequently. Remove the bowl from the heat and scrape the melted chocolate into a clean bowl.

3 Cut out a 23cm/9in square piece of baking parchment. Grease one side and 5cm/2in of the base of an 18cm/7in square cake tin (pan). Fold the paper in half and fit the crease line into the greased corner of the tin so the side and part of the base and ends are lined.

4 Stir the biscuits into the white chocolate mix followed by the chocolate mint sticks. Add the milk chocolate, stir to combine then turn the mixture into the lined section of the tin. Hold the tin at an angle, then level the surface of the chocolate. Chill, propping the tin up with another container to maintain the angle to form the pyramid shape. Leave for 2 hours, until set.

5 Remove the cake from the tin, place on a flat plate and peel off the paper. In their wrappers, crush the mints with a rolling pin. Melt the reserved white chocolate in a heatproof bowl set over a pan of hot water. Then spread the white chocolate over the top sloping side of the pyramid, sprinkle with the crushed mints and press in lightly.

Nutritional information per cookie: Energy 234kcal/977kJ; Protein 3.2g; Carbohydrate 24.8g, of which sugars 21.5g; Fat 14.2g, of which saturates 8.4g; Cholesterol 11mg; Calcium 100mg; Fibre 0.2g; Sodium 63mg.

Almond-scented chocolate cherry wedges

These cookies are a chocoholic's dream, and use the very best quality chocolate. Erratically shaped, they are packed with crunchy cookies, juicy raisins and munchy nuts.

MAKES ABOUT 15

50g/2oz ratafia biscuits (almond macaroons) or small amaretti
90g/3¹/₂oz shortcake biscuits (cookies)
150g/5oz/1 cup jumbo raisins
50g/2oz/¹/₄ cup undyed glacé (candied) cherries, quartered
450g/1lb dark (bittersweet) chocolate (minimum 70 per cent cocoa solids)
90g/3¹/₂oz/scant ¹/₂ cup unsalted (sweet) butter, diced
30ml/2 tbsp amaretto liqueur (optional)
25g/1oz/¹/₄ cup toasted flaked (sliced) almonds

1 Line a baking sheet with baking parchment. Put the ratafia biscuits or amaretti in a bowl. Leave half whole and break the remainder into pieces. Break each of the shortcake biscuits into three or four pieces and add to the bowl. Add the raisins and cherries and toss together.

2 Melt the chocolate and butter with the liqueur, if using, in the microwave or in a heatproof bowl set over a pan of hot water. When the chocolate has melted, remove from the heat and stir the mixture until combined and smooth. Set aside to cool slightly.

3 Pour the chocolate over the biscuit mixture and toss lightly together until everything is coated in chocolate. Spread out over the prepared baking sheet.

4 Sprinkle over the almonds and push them in at angles so they stick well to the chocolate-coated biscuits.

5 When the chocolate mixture is completely set, use a sharp knife to cut or break into shapes with your fingers, as you wish, such as long thin triangles, stumpy squares or irregular shapes and serve.

Nutritional information per cookie: Energy 288kcal/1206kJ; Protein 2.7g; Carbohydrate 34.6g, of which sugars 29.7g; Fat 16.4g, of which saturates 9.5g; Cholesterol 20mg; Calcium 31mg; Fibre 1.3g; Sodium 75mg.

Nutty marshmallow and chocolate squares

*Unashamedly sweet, with chocolate, marshmallows, cherries, nuts and coconut, this recipe is a
favourite with children of all ages, and sweet-toothed adults too.*

MAKES 9

200g/7oz digestive biscuits
   (graham crackers)
90g/3¹/₂oz plain (semisweet) chocolate
200g/7oz mini coloured marshmallows
150g/5oz/1¹/₄ cups chopped walnuts
90g/3¹/₂oz/scant ¹/₂ cup glacé (candied)
   cherries, halved
50g/2oz/²/₃ cup sweetened desiccated
   (dry shredded) coconut
350g/12oz milk chocolate

1 Put the biscuits in a polythene bag
and crush them with a rolling pin
into small pieces. Place in a bowl.

2 Melt the plain chocolate in a
heatproof bowl set over a pan of
hot water. Pour the melted plain
chocolate over the broken biscuits
and stir well. Spread the mixture
evenly in the base of a 20cm/8in
square shallow cake tin (pan).

3 Put the marshmallows, walnuts,
cherries and coconut in a bowl. Melt
the milk chocolate in a heatproof
bowl set over a pan of hot water.

4 Pour the melted chocolate over
the mixture and toss together until
almost everything is coated. Spread
the mixture over the chocolate
base, but leave in chunky lumps.
Chill, then cut into squares to serve.

Nutritional information per cookie: Energy 603kcal/2523kJ; Protein 8.6g; Carbohydrate 69.7g, of which sugars 53.2g;
Fat 34.1g, of which saturates 14.7g; Cholesterol 19mg; Calcium 133mg; Fibre 2.5g; Sodium 179mg.

Chocolate nut slice

Children of all ages will love this combination of broken cookies, chocolate and nuts. Although the unsliced bar looks small, it's very rich so is best sliced very thinly. If you have any other plain cookies in the cupboard you can use them instead of the rich tea, with equally good results.

MAKES 10 SLICES

225g/8oz milk chocolate

40g/1½oz/3 tbsp unsalted (sweet) butter, diced

75g/3oz rich tea biscuits (plain cookies)

50g/2oz/½ cup flaked (sliced) almonds

75g/3oz plain (semisweet) or white chocolate, roughly chopped

icing (confectioners') sugar, for dusting

1 Break the milk chocolate into pieces and place in a heatproof bowl with the butter. Rest the bowl over a pan of simmering water and stir frequently until melted.

2 Meanwhile, dampen a 450g/1lb loaf tin (pan) and line the base and sides with clear film (plastic wrap). Don't worry about smoothing out the creases in the film.

3 When the chocolate has melted, remove it from the heat and leave for 5 minutes until slightly cooled.

4 Break the biscuits into small pieces, then stir into the melted chocolate with the almonds. Add the chopped chocolate to the bowl and fold in quickly and lightly.

5 Turn the mixture into the tin and pack down with a fork. Tap the base of the tin gently on the work surface. Chill for 2 hours until set.

6 To serve, turn the chocolate loaf on to a board and peel away the clear film. Dust lightly with icing sugar and slice thinly.

Nutritional information per cookie: Energy 248kcal/1034kJ; Protein 3.7g; Carbohydrate 23.5g, of which sugars 19.4g; Fat 16.1g, of which saturates 8.2g; Cholesterol 16mg; Calcium 74mg; Fibre 0.9g; Sodium 75mg.

Chocolate birds' nests

These delightful crispy chocolate nests make a perfect Easter treat and are a real favourite with kids. They're so quick and easy to make and even young children can have great fun shaping the chocolate mixture inside the paper cases and tucking the pastel-coloured eggs inside the nests.

MAKES 12

200g/7oz milk chocolate
25g/1oz/2 tbsp unsalted (sweet)
   butter, diced

90g/3½oz Shredded Wheat cereal
36 small pastel-coloured, sugar-coated
   chocolate eggs

1 Line the sections of a tartlet tray (muffin pan) with 12 decorative paper cake cases.

2 Break the milk chocolate into pieces and put in a bowl with the butter. Rest the bowl over a pan of gently simmering water and stir frequently until melted. Remove the bowl from the heat and leave to cool for a few minutes.

3 Using your fingers, crumble the Shredded Wheat into the melted chocolate. Stir well until the cereal is completely coated in chocolate.

4 Divide the mixture among the paper cases, pressing it down gently with the back of a spoon and make a slight indentation in the centre. Tuck three eggs into each nest and leave to set for about 2 hours before serving.

COOK'S TIP
Bags of sugar-coated chocolate eggs are widely available in supermarkets at Easter time. However, if you have trouble finding them out of season, try an old-fashioned sweet store. Often they have large jars of this type of sweet (candy), which they sell all year round.

Nutritional information per cookie: Energy 214kcal/896kJ; Protein 3.4g; Carbohydrate 24.4g, of which sugars 19g; Fat 12.1g, of which saturates 7.2g; Cholesterol 12mg; Calcium 77mg; Fibre 1g; Sodium 42mg.

Sweet peanut wafers

These delicate wafers make a fun, no-bake recipe that kids can help with. Just remember to chill the wafers after they have been assembled, otherwise they will be almost impossible to cut.

MAKES 12

65g/2¹/₂oz/4 tbsp unsalted (sweet) butter, at room temperature, diced
65g/2¹/₂oz/generous ¹/₂ cup icing (confectioners') sugar
115g/4oz/¹/₂ cup crunchy peanut butter
12 fan-shaped wafers
50g/2oz plain (semisweet) chocolate, broken into pieces

1 Put the butter and sugar in a bowl and beat with a hand-held electric whisk until very light and creamy. Beat in the peanut butter.

2 Spread a thick layer of the mixture on to a wafer and spread to the edges. Place another wafer on top and press it down gently. Spread the top wafer with more buttercream, then place another wafer on top and press down.

3 Use the remaining buttercream and wafers to assemble three more fans in the same way. Spread any remaining buttercream around the sides of the fans. Chill for at least 30 minutes until firm.

4 Carefully slice each fan into three equal wedges and arrange in a single layer on a small tray. Melt the chocolate in a heatproof bowl set over a pan of simmering water, then leave to cool for a few minutes. Drizzle lines of chocolate over the wafers, then leave to set in a cool place for at least 1 hour.

Nutritional information per cookie: Energy 184kcal/769kJ; Protein 3.7g; Carbohydrate 19.4g, of which sugars 9.1g; Fat 10.7g, of which saturates 4.8g; Cholesterol 12mg; Calcium 30mg; Fibre 0.6g; Sodium 79mg.

Chocolate crispy cookies

These little chocolate-coated cornflake cakes couldn't be easier to make and so are great for young aspiring cooks who want to get involved in the kitchen.

MAKES 10

90g/3¹/₂oz milk chocolate
15ml/1 tbsp golden (light corn) syrup
90g/3¹/₂oz/4¹/₂ cups cornflakes
icing (confectioners') sugar, for dusting

1 Line a large baking sheet with baking parchment. Break the chocolate into a heatproof bowl and add the syrup. Rest the bowl over a pan of gently simmering water and leave until melted, stirring frequently. Put the cornflakes in a plastic bag and, using a rolling pin, lightly crush the cornflakes, breaking them into fairly small pieces.

2 Remove the bowl from the heat and tip in the cornflakes. Mix well until the cornflakes are thoroughly coated in the chocolate mixture. Place a 6.5cm/2¹/₂in round cutter on the paper and put a spoonful of the chocolate mixture in the centre. Pack down firmly to make a thick cookie.

3 Ease away the cutter and continue making cookies until all the mixture has been used up. Chill for 1 hour.

4 Put a little icing sugar in a bowl. Lift each cookie from the paper and roll the edges in the icing sugar to finish.

Nutritional information per cookie: Energy 84kcal/355kJ; Protein 1.4g; Carbohydrate 14.2g, of which sugars 7.2g; Fat 2.8g, of which saturates 1.7g; Cholesterol 2mg; Calcium 21mg; Fibre 0.2g; Sodium 112mg.

White chocolate snowballs

These little spherical cookies are particularly popular during the Christmas season. They're simple to make, yet utterly delicious and bursting with creamy, buttery flavours. If you like, make them in advance of a special tea as they will keep well in the refrigerator for a few days.

MAKES 16

200g/7oz white chocolate
25g/1oz/2 tbsp butter, diced
90g/3¹/₂oz/generous 1 cup desiccated (dry unsweetened shredded) coconut
90g/3¹/₂oz syrup sponge or Madeira cake
icing (confectioners') sugar, for dusting

1 Break the chocolate into pieces and put in a heatproof bowl with the butter. Set the bowl over a pan of simmering water and stir frequently until melted. Set aside to cool for a few minutes.

2 Put 50g/2oz/²/₃ cup of the coconut on a plate. Crumble the cake and add to the melted chocolate with the remaining coconut. Mix to a chunky paste.

3 Take spoonfuls of the mixture and roll into balls, about 2.5cm/1in in diameter.

4 Immediately roll the balls in the reserved coconut and place on baking parchment. Leave them to set.

5 Once the snowballs are set, dust them with plenty of icing sugar and serve.

Nutritional information per cookie: Energy 133kcal/554kJ; Protein 1.6g; Carbohydrate 10.9g, of which sugars 9.7g; Fat 9.5g, of which saturates 6.6g; Cholesterol 3mg; Calcium 38mg; Fibre 0.8g; Sodium 46mg.

Apricot and coconut kisses

These tangy, fruity treats make a colourful addition to the tea table. Although they are easy to make and can be mixed and shaped in a matter of a few minutes, remember to allow plenty of time for the apricots to soak, and also for the kisses to chill before serving.

MAKES 12

130g/4¹/₂oz/generous ¹/₂ cup
    ready-to-eat dried apricots
100ml/3¹/₂fl oz/scant ¹/₂ cup
    orange juice
40g/1¹/₂oz/3 tbsp unsalted (sweet)
    butter, at room temperature, diced
75g/3oz/³/₄ cup icing
    (confectioners') sugar
90g/3¹/₂oz/generous 1 cup desiccated
    (dry unsweetened shredded) coconut,
    lightly toasted
2 glacé (candied) cherries, cut
    into wedges

1 Finely chop the dried apricots, then tip them into a bowl. Pour in the orange juice and leave to soak for about 1 hour until all the juice has been absorbed.

2 In a large bowl, beat together the butter and sugar with a wooden spoon until pale and creamy.

3 Gradually add the soaked apricots to the creamed butter mixture, beating well after each addition, then stir in the toasted coconut.

4 Line a small baking tray with baking parchment.

5 Place teaspoonfuls of the coconut mixture on to the paper, piling them up into little pyramid shapes. Gently press the mixture together with your fingers to form neat shapes.

6 Top each kiss with a tiny wedge of cherry, gently pressing it into the mixture. Chill the kisses for about 1 hour until firm, then serve.

Nutritional information per cookie: Energy 115kcal/480kJ; Protein 1g; Carbohydrate 11.7g, of which sugars 11.7g; Fat 7.5g, of which saturates 5.7g; Cholesterol 7mg; Calcium 14mg; Fibre 1.7g; Sodium 25mg.

Pink piggies

These are what you could call rainy day cookies. They are fun to make and thoroughly absorbing when the family is stuck indoors. You might want to make up icings in other colours and experiment with your own animal variations. Children's books are a great source of inspiration.

MAKES 10

90g/3½oz/1 cup icing (confectioners')
   sugar, plus extra for dusting
50g/2oz/¼ cup unsalted (sweet)
   butter, at room temperature, diced
10 rich tea (plain cookies) or digestive
   biscuits (graham crackers)

200g/7oz white ready-to-roll icing
pink food colouring
small, pink soft sweets (candies)
tube of black writer icing

1 For the buttercream, put the icing sugar and butter in a bowl and beat with a hand-held electric whisk until smooth, pale and creamy. Spread the biscuits almost to the edges with the buttercream.

2 Reserve 25g/1oz of the ready-to-roll icing and add a few drops of the pink food colouring to the remainder. Knead on a work surface that has been lightly dusted with icing sugar until the pink colouring is evenly distributed.

3 Reserve 25g/1oz of the pink icing. If necessary, lightly dust your work surface with more icing sugar and roll out the remaining pink icing thinly.

4 Using a cookie cutter that is just slightly smaller than the biscuits, cut out rounds of pink icing. Lay a round over each biscuit and press it down on to the buttercream.

5 Halve five of the pink sweets and press into an oval shape. Make two small holes in each one with a wooden skewer to make a nose. Using a little of the buttercream, attach a halved sweet to the centre of each cookie. Using the black writer icing, pipe two small dots of icing above the nose to resemble eyes, then pipe a small, curved mouth.

6 Thinly roll out the reserved pink icing and the reserved white icing. Dampen the white icing with a little water and press the pink icing on top. Cut out triangles for ears. Dampen one edge of the ears with a little water and secure, pink side up, to the cookies. Gently curl the ears out at the ends.

Nutritional information per cookie: Energy 188kcal/794kJ; Protein 1g; Carbohydrate 33g, of which sugars 25.8g; Fat 6.8g, of which saturates 3.8g; Cholesterol 16mg; Calcium 25mg; Fibre 0.3g; Sodium 110mg.

"Free from" and healthy cookies

Food intolerances, allergies and health

problems need not deprive you of the

pleasures of eating home-made cookies.

You will be amazed by the range of

low-fat, dairy-free, reduced-sugar or

gluten-free treats you can make — and

what's more, they're so delicious, the

whole family will be clamouring for them.

Carob chip shorties

Perfect for anyone on a gluten-free or cow's-milk-free diet, these lovely cookies are best eaten freshly made, preferably while still slightly warm from the oven.

MAKES 12

175g/6oz/1½ cups gluten-free flour
25g/1oz/2 tbsp soft light brown sugar
75g/3oz/6 tbsp vegetable margarine
50g/2oz/⅓ cup carob chips
15–25ml/1–1½ tbsp clear
    honey, warmed
demerara (raw) or caster (superfine)
    sugar, for sprinkling

1 Preheat the oven to 160°C/ 325°F/Gas 3. Line two baking sheets with baking parchment.

2 Put the flour and brown sugar in a large bowl. Add the margarine and rub it in with your fingertips. Add the carob chips, then stir in just enough warmed honey to bring the mixture together, but not make it sticky.

3 Roll the dough out between two sheets of baking parchment to about 8mm/⅓in thick.

4 Stamp out rounds using a plain 5cm/2in round cutter. Place on the baking sheets. Prick each cookie with a fork and sprinkle with sugar.

5 Bake for about 15–20 minutes, or until firm. Cool on a wire rack.

Nutritional information per cookie: Energy 133kcal/553kJ; Protein 1.2g; Carbohydrate 17.5g, of which sugars 5.8g; Fat 6.4g, of which saturates 2.9g; Cholesterol 1mg; Calcium 6mg; Fibre 0.4g; Sodium 51mg.

Fruit and millet treacle cookies

These little cookies are quick to make, and will no doubt disappear just as quickly when they come out of the oven. They are gluten- and cow's milk-free.

MAKES ABOUT 25–30

90g/3¹/₂oz/7 tbsp
   vegetable margarine
150g/5oz/²/₃ cup light muscovado
   (brown) sugar
30ml/2 tbsp black treacle (molasses)
1 egg
150g/5oz/1¹/₄ cups gluten-free flour
50g/2oz/¹/₂ cup millet flakes
50g/2oz/¹/₂ cup almonds, chopped
200g/7oz/generous 1 cup luxury
   mixed dried fruit

1 Preheat the oven to 190°C/ 375°F/Gas 5. Line two large baking sheets with baking parchment.

2 Put the margarine, muscovado sugar, treacle and egg in a large bowl and beat together until well combined. (The mixture should be light and fluffy.)

3 Stir in the flour and millet flakes, the almonds and dried fruit. Put tablespoonfuls of the mixture on to the prepared baking sheets.

4 Bake for about 15 minutes until brown. Leave on the baking sheets for a few minutes, then transfer to a wire rack to cool completely.

Nutritional information per cookie: Energy 99kcal/416kJ; Protein 1.2g; Carbohydrate 15.8g, of which sugars 10.5g; Fat 3.7g, of which saturates 1.2g; Cholesterol 7mg; Calcium 20mg; Fibre 0.4g; Sodium 32mg.

Double chocolate slices

These delicious gluten-free cookies have a smooth chocolate base, topped with a mint-flavoured cream and drizzles of melted chocolate. Perfect for a teatime treat – or at any time of day.

MAKES 12

200g/7oz/1³/₄ cups gluten-free flour
25g/1oz/2 tbsp unsweetened
    cocoa powder
150g/5oz/²/₃ cup unsalted (sweet)
    butter, cut into small pieces
75g/3oz/³/₄ cup icing
    (confectioners') sugar

FOR THE TOPPING

75g/3oz white chocolate mint crisps
50g/2oz/¹/₄ cup unsalted (sweet)
    butter, softened
90g/3¹/₂oz/scant 1 cup icing
    (confectioners') sugar
50g/2oz gluten-free milk chocolate

1 Preheat the oven to 180°C/350°F/Gas 4. Grease an 18cm/7in square shallow baking tin (pan) and line with a strip of baking parchment that comes up over two opposite sides.

2 Put the flour and cocoa powder into a food processor and add the butter. Process until the mixture resembles fine breadcrumbs. Add the icing sugar and process to form a smooth soft dough. Turn the dough into the tin and press out to the edges to make an even layer. Bake for 25 minutes, then remove from the oven and leave the base to cool completely in the tin.

3 For the topping, put the chocolate mint crisps in a plastic bag and tap with a rolling pin until they are crushed. Beat the butter and sugar together until creamy, then beat in the crushed crisps. Spread evenly over the base.

4 Melt the milk chocolate in a small heatproof bowl set over a pan of hot water. Lift the base out of the tin; remove the paper. Using a teaspoon, drizzle the melted chocolate over the topping. Leave to set, then cut into squares.

Nutritional information per cookie: Energy 299kcal/1248kJ; Protein 2.3g; Carbohydrate 34.4g, of which sugars 20.8g; Fat 17.3g, of which saturates 10.8g; Cholesterol 37mg; Calcium 28mg; Fibre 0.8g; Sodium 126mg.

Meringue squiggles

Free from gluten, wheat and cow's milk, these wiggly wands are great for children's parties. They are fun to shape and eat, and kids of all ages love making and decorating them.

MAKES 14–16

2 egg whites
90g/3¹/₂oz/¹/₂ cup caster
(superfine) sugar
45ml/3 tbsp icing (confectioners') sugar
multi-coloured sugar sprinkles,
to decorate

1 Preheat the oven to 150°C/300°F/Gas 2. Line a large baking sheet with baking parchment. Put the egg whites in a clean bowl and whisk until firm peaks form. Add a spoonful of caster sugar to the whisked egg whites and whisk for 15 seconds to combine. Add another spoonful and whisk again. Continue in this way until all the sugar has been added.

2 Spoon the meringue mixture into a piping (pastry) bag fitted with a large plain nozzle. Pipe wavy lines of meringue, about 13cm/5in long, on to the baking sheet and bake for about 1 hour until dry and crisp. Carefully peel the meringues off the baking parchment and transfer to a wire rack to cool.

3 Put the icing sugar in a bowl and mix in a few drops of water to make a smooth paste. Brush the tops of the meringues with a little of the sugar paste, then scatter over the multi-coloured sugar sprinkles to decorate.

Nutritional information per cookie: Energy 35kcal/148kJ; Protein 0.4g; Carbohydrate 8.8g, of which sugars 8.8g; Fat 0g, of which saturates 0g; Cholesterol 0mg; Calcium 5mg; Fibre 0g; Sodium 8mg.

Rocky road wedges

Free from gluten and wheat, these crumbly wedges contain homemade popcorn in place of broken cookies, which are the classic ingredient in no-bake cookies such as this.

MAKES 8

15ml/1 tbsp vegetable oil
25g/1oz/2¹/2 tbsp popping corn
150g/5oz orange-flavoured plain
   (semisweet) chocolate, broken
   into pieces

25g/1oz/2 tbsp unsalted (sweet)
   butter, diced
75g/3oz soft vanilla fudge, diced
icing (confectioners') sugar, for dusting

1 Heat the oil in a pan. Add the popping corn, cover and heat, shaking the pan once or twice, until the popping noises die down. (Don't lift the lid until the popping stops.)

2 Remove from the heat and leave for 30 seconds before removing the lid. Be careful, as there may be quite a lot of steam trapped inside. Transfer the popcorn to a bowl and leave to cool for about 5 minutes.

3 Line the base of an 18cm/7in sandwich tin (pan). Once cooled, tip the popcorn into a plastic bag and tap with a rolling pin to break up into pieces.

4 Melt the chocolate and butter together in a heatproof bowl set over a pan of simmering water, stirring frequently. Leave to cool for 2 minutes.

5 Stir the popcorn and fudge into the chocolate until coated, then turn the mixture into the tin and press down firmly. Leave to set for 30 minutes. Turn out on to a board and cut into wedges. Serve lightly dusted with sugar.

Nutritional information per cookie: Energy 191kcal/798kJ; Protein 1.5g; Carbohydrate 21g, of which sugars 19.3g; Fat 11.8g, of which saturates 5.9g; Cholesterol 11mg; Calcium 19mg; Fibre 0.5g; Sodium 33mg.

Big Macs

These giant macaroons are crisp on the outside, chewy in the middle and naturally free from gluten and cow's milk. Ground almonds make a great alternative to wheat flour.

MAKES 9

2 egg whites
5ml/1 tsp almond extract
115g/4oz/1 cup ground almonds
130g/4½oz/generous 1 cup light muscovado (brown) sugar

1 Preheat the oven to 180°C/350°F/Gas 4. Line a large baking sheet with baking parchment. Put the egg whites in a large, clean bowl and whisk until they form stiff peaks.

2 Add the almond extract to the egg whites and whisk to combine. Sprinkle over the ground almonds and sugar and gently fold in using a metal spoon.

3 Place nine spoonfuls of the mixture, spacing them well apart, on to the baking sheet and flatten slightly. Bake for 15 minutes until risen, deep golden and beginning to turn crisp.

4 Leave the macaroons on the baking sheets for 5 minutes, then transfer to a wire rack to cool.

Nutritional information per cookie: Energy 138kcal/577kJ; Protein 3.4g; Carbohydrate 16g, of which sugars 15.6g; Fat 7.1g, of which saturates 0.6g; Cholesterol 0mg; Calcium 39mg; Fibre 0.9g; Sodium 16mg.

Cashew nut button cookies

These light little cookies, flavoured with ground cashew nuts, are coated in toasted hazelnuts.
They are suitable for people on gluten-free and cow's-milk-free diets.

MAKES ABOUT 20

1 egg white
25g/1oz/2 tbsp caster
    (superfine) sugar
150g/5oz/1¼ cups unroasted cashew
    nuts, ground
50g/2oz/⅓ cup dates, finely chopped
5ml/1 tsp finely grated
    orange rind
30ml/2 tbsp pure maple or
    maple-flavoured syrup
90g/3½oz/scant 1 cup toasted
    hazelnuts, chopped

1 Preheat the oven to 190°C/375°F/Gas 5. Line two baking sheets with baking parchment.

2 In a bowl, whisk the egg white until stiff. Whisk in the sugar. Stir in the cashews, dates, orange rind and syrup. Mix well. Put the chopped hazelnuts in a small bowl.

3 Drop small spoonfuls of the cookie mixture into the hazelnuts and toss until well coated.

4 Place on the prepared baking sheets and bake for about 10 minutes until lightly browned. Leave to cool on the baking sheets.

Nutritional information per cookie: Energy 92kcal/382kJ; Protein 2.4g; Carbohydrate 5.9g, of which sugars 4.8g; Fat 6.7g, of which saturates 1g; Cholesterol 0mg; Calcium 11mg; Fibre 0.6g; Sodium 29mg.

Shortbread ring cookies

Decorated with chopped sweets, these gluten- and dairy-free cookies are great for younger kids. Don't forget to check the ingredients on the jellied sweets to make sure they are gluten-free.

MAKES 8–10

150g/5oz/1¼ cups gluten-free flour
90g/3½oz/½ cup rice flour
finely grated rind of 1 lemon
75g/3oz/6 tbsp dairy-free margarine
50g/2oz/¼ cup caster (superfine) sugar
1 egg yolk
10ml/2 tsp water

FOR THE TOPPING

90g/3½oz/scant 1 cup icing
   (confectioners') sugar
50g/2oz/½ cup dairy-free margarine
small jellied fruit sweets (candies)

1 Put the flours, lemon rind and margarine in a food processor and process to combine. Add the sugar, egg yolk and water and mix to a dough. Turn the dough on to a floured surface and knead. Wrap and chill for 30 minutes.

2 Preheat the oven to 180°C/350°F/Gas 4. Grease a baking sheet. Roll out the dough on a lightly floured surface to a thickness of about 5mm/¼in.

3 Using a 6.5cm/2¾in plain or fluted cutter, cut out rounds and place on the baking sheet. Using a 4cm/1½in round cutter, cut out and remove the centre of each round. Bake for about 20 minutes until beginning to turn pale golden. Leave for 2 minutes, then transfer to a wire rack to cool.

4 For the topping, put the icing sugar and margarine in a bowl and beat until creamy. Pipe or spoon the topping on to the ring cookies. Chop the sweets into small pieces and gently press them into the cream to decorate.

Nutritional information per cookie: Energy 242kcal/1008kJ; Protein 1.9g; Carbohydrate 34g, of which sugars 14.8g; Fat 10.9g, of which saturates 4.6g; Cholesterol 22mg; Calcium 16mg; Fibre 0.5g; Sodium 103mg.

Apricot and pecan flapjack

A tried-and-tested favourite made even more delicious by the addition of maple syrup, fruit and nuts. This is a real energy booster at any time of day for kids and adults alike.

MAKES 10

150g/5oz/²⁄₃ cup unsalted (sweet) butter, diced
150g/5oz/²⁄₃ cup light muscovado (brown) sugar
30ml/2 tbsp maple syrup
200g/7oz/2 cups rolled oats
50g/2oz/¹⁄₂ cup pecan nuts, chopped
50g/2oz/¹⁄₄ cup ready-to-eat dried apricots, chopped

1 Preheat the oven to 160°C/325°F/Gas 3. Lightly grease an 18cm/7in square shallow baking tin (pan). Put the butter, sugar and maple syrup in a large heavy pan and heat gently until the butter has melted. Remove from the heat and stir in the oats, nuts and apricots until well combined.

2 Spread evenly in the prepared tin and, using a knife, score the mixture into ten bars. Bake for about 25–30 minutes, or until golden.

3 Remove from the oven and cut through the scored lines. Leave until completely cold before removing from the tin.

Nutritional information per cookie: Energy 240kcal/1000kJ; Protein 3.2g; Carbohydrate 18.3g, of which sugars 3.7g; Fat 17.6g, of which saturates 8.1g; Cholesterol 32mg; Calcium 21mg; Fibre 1.9g; Sodium 98mg.

Luxury muesli cookies

It is best to use a "luxury" muesli for this recipe, preferably one with 50 per cent mixed cereal and 50 per cent fruit, nuts and seeds. These buttery, crunchy cookies are ideal for a snack at any time.

MAKES ABOUT 20

115g/4oz/¹/₂ cup unsalted
  (sweet) butter
45ml/3 tbsp golden (light corn) syrup
115g/4oz/¹/₂ cup demerara
  (raw) sugar

175g/6oz/1¹/₂ cups "luxury"
  muesli (granola)
90g/3¹/₂oz/³/₄ cup self-raising
  (self-rising) flour
5ml/1 tsp ground cinnamon

1 Preheat the oven to 160°C/325°F/Gas 3. Line two or three baking sheets with baking parchment.

2 Put the butter, syrup and sugar in a large pan and heat gently. Stir constantly until the butter has completely melted.

3 Remove the pan from the heat then stir in the muesli, flour and cinnamon and mix together well. Set aside to cool slightly.

4 Place spoonfuls of the mixture, slightly apart, on the baking sheets. Bake for 15 minutes until the cookies are just beginning to brown around the edges.

5 Leave to cool for a few minutes on the baking sheets, then carefully transfer to a wire rack to cool completely.

VARIATION
Tropical muesli containing coconut and dried tropical fruits makes an interesting alternative to regular luxury muesli.

Nutritional information per cookie: Energy 120kcal/502kJ; Protein 1.4g; Carbohydrate 17.2g, of which sugars 9.3g; Fat 5.5g, of which saturates 3.1g; Cholesterol 12mg; Calcium 15mg; Fibre 0.8g; Sodium 46mg.

Low-fat orange oaties

These are so delicious that it is difficult to believe that they are healthy too. As they are packed with flavour and wonderfully crunchy, the whole family will love them.

MAKES ABOUT 16

175g/6oz/³/₄ cup clear honey
120ml/4fl oz/¹/₂ cup orange juice
90g/3¹/₂oz/1 cup rolled oats,
   lightly toasted
115g/4oz/1 cup plain (all-purpose) flour
115g/4oz/generous ¹/₂ cup golden caster
   (superfine) sugar
finely grated rind of 1 orange
5ml/1 tsp bicarbonate of soda
   (baking soda)

1 Preheat the oven to 180°C/350°F/Gas 4. Line two large baking sheets with baking parchment.

2 Put the honey and orange juice in a small pan and simmer over a low heat for 8–10 minutes, stirring occasionally, until the mixture is thick and syrupy.

3 Put the oats, flour, sugar and orange rind into a bowl.

4 Mix the bicarbonate of soda with 15ml/1 tbsp boiling water and add to the flour mixture, together with the honey syrup. Mix well.

5 Place spoonfuls of the mixture on to the prepared baking sheets, spaced slightly apart, and bake for 10–12 minutes, or until golden brown. Leave to cool on the sheets for 5 minutes before transferring to a wire rack to cool completely.

Nutritional information per cookie: Energy 110kcal/466kJ; Protein 1.5g; Carbohydrate 26.2g, of which sugars 16.6g; Fat 0.6g, of which saturates 0g; Cholesterol 0mg; Calcium 18mg; Fibre 0.6g; Sodium 4mg.

Very low-fat brownies

If you ever need proof that you can still enjoy sweet treats even when you are on a low-fat diet, here it is. These brownies are not just tasty, but also very quick and easy to make.

MAKES 16

100g/3³/₄oz/scant 1 cup plain
(all-purpose) flour
2.5ml/¹/₂ tsp baking powder
45ml/3 tbsp unsweetened
cocoa powder
200g/7oz/1 cup caster (superfine) sugar

100ml/3¹/₂fl oz/scant ¹/₂ cup natural
(plain) low-fat yogurt
2 eggs, beaten
5ml/1 tsp vanilla extract
25ml/1¹/₂ tbsp vegetable oil

1 Preheat the oven to 180°C/350°F/Gas 4. Line a 20cm/8in square cake tin (pan) with baking parchment.

2 Sift the flour, baking powder and cocoa powder into a bowl. Stir in the caster sugar, then beat in the yogurt, eggs, vanilla and vegetable oil until thoroughly combined. Put the mixture into the prepared tin.

3 Bake for about 25 minutes until just firm to the touch. Leave in the tin until cooled completely.

4 Using a sharp knife, cut the brownies into 16 squares, then remove from the tin using a spatula.

Nutritional information per cookie: Energy 53kcal/222kJ; Protein 2.2g; Carbohydrate 5.7g, of which sugars 0.6g; Fat 2.6g, of which saturates 0.7g; Cholesterol 24mg; Calcium 28mg; Fibre 0.5g; Sodium 41mg.

Chewy flapjacks

Flapjacks are about the easiest cookies to make and, with a little guidance, can be put together in a matter of minutes by even the youngest cooks.

MAKES 18

250g/9oz/generous 1 cup unsalted
　(sweet) butter
finely grated rind of 1 large orange
225g/8oz/²/₃ cup golden
　(light corn) syrup
75g/3oz/¹/₃ cup light muscovado
　(brown) sugar
375g/13oz/3³/₄ cups rolled oats

1 Preheat the oven to 180°C/ 350°F/Gas 4. Line the base and sides of a 28 x 20cm/11 x 8in shallow baking tin (pan) with baking parchment.

2 Put the butter, orange rind, syrup and sugar in a large pan and heat gently until the butter has melted.

3 Add the oats to the pan and stir to mix thoroughly. Tip the mixture into the tin and spread into the corners in an even layer.

4 Bake for 15–20 minutes until just beginning to colour around the edges. (The mixture will still be very soft but will harden as it cools.) Leave to cool completely in the tin.

5 Lift the flapjack out of the tin in one piece and cut into fingers.

Nutritional information per cookie: Energy 241kcal/1007kJ; Protein 2.7g; Carbohydrate 29.5g, of which sugars 14.3g; Fat 13.2g, of which saturates 7.2g; Cholesterol 30mg; Calcium 18mg; Fibre 1.4g; Sodium 125mg.

Iced carob cookies

If you are unable to eat chocolate but still crave it, these heavenly cookies, with their creamy topping, provide the answer to your wishes.

MAKES 12–16

115g/4oz/¹/₂ cup butter
10ml/2 tsp carob powder
115g/4oz/1 cup wholemeal
   (whole-wheat) flour
5ml/1 tsp baking powder
75g/3oz/¹/₃ cup muscovado
   (molasses) sugar
50g/2oz/generous ¹/₂ cup rolled oats

FOR THE TOPPING

50g/2oz carob bar, coarsely chopped
45ml/3 tbsp double (heavy) cream
15ml/1 tbsp chopped ready-to-eat
   dried apricots

1 Preheat the oven to 190°C/375°F/Gas 5. Then line the base and sides of an 18cm/7in square shallow cake tin (pan) with baking parchment. Put the butter in a large pan and add the carob powder. Stir over a low heat until the mixture is smooth and combined. Stir in the remaining ingredients and mix together well.

2 Press the mixture into the prepared tin and bake for about 20–25 minutes until just set. Mark into squares or bars while still hot. Leave to cool in the tin.

3 To make the topping, stir the carob and cream in a small pan over a low heat. Spread over the cookies and sprinkle the apricots on top.

Nutritional information per cookie: Energy 140kcal/585kJ; Protein 1.7g; Carbohydrate 14.3g, of which sugars 7.4g; Fat 8.9g, of which saturates 5.3g; Cholesterol 19mg; Calcium 12mg; Fibre 1.1g; Sodium 52mg.

Tropical fruit slice

Densely packed dried exotic fruits make the filling for these deliciously moist bars. They make a popular after-school snack for hungry kids, or pop one into their lunch box as a surprise.

MAKES 12–16

175g/6oz/1¹/₂ cups plain
   (all-purpose) flour
90g/3¹/₂oz/generous ¹/₂ cup white
   vegetable fat (shortening)
60ml/4 tbsp apricot jam, sieved, or
   ready-made apricot glaze

FOR THE FILLING
115g/4oz/¹/₂ cup unsalted (sweet)
   butter, softened

115g/4oz/generous ¹/₂ cup caster
   (superfine) sugar
1 egg, beaten
25g/1oz/¹/₄ cup ground almonds
25g/1oz/2¹/₂ tbsp ground rice
300g/11oz/scant 2 cups ready-to-eat
   mixed dried tropical fruits, chopped

1 Preheat the oven to 180°C/350°F/Gas 4. Lightly grease a 28 x 18cm/11 x 7in tin (pan). Put the flour and vegetable fat in a bowl and rub in with your fingers until the mixture resembles fine breadcrumbs. Add enough water to mix to a firm dough.

2 Roll out on a lightly floured surface and use to line the base of the prepared tin. Spread 30ml/2 tbsp of the jam or glaze over the dough.

3 To make the filling, cream together the butter and sugar until light and creamy. Beat in the egg, then stir in the almonds, rice and mixed fruits. Spread the mixture evenly in the tin.

4 Bake for about 35 minutes. Remove from the oven and brush with the remaining jam or glaze. Leave to cool completely in the tin before cutting into bars.

Nutritional information per cookie: Energy 220kcal/921kJ; Protein 2.7g; Carbohydrate 26.9g, of which sugars 17.3g; Fat 12g, of which saturates 6g; Cholesterol 28mg; Calcium 41mg; Fibre 1.7g; Sodium 98mg.

Fruity breakfast bars

Instead of buying fruit and cereal bars from the supermarket, try making this quick and easy version – they are much tastier and more nutritious than most of the commercially-made ones.

MAKES 12

270g/10oz jar apple sauce

115g/4oz/¹⁄₂ cup ready-to-eat dried
 apricots, chopped

115g/4oz/³⁄₄ cup raisins

50g/2oz/¹⁄₄ cup demerara (raw) sugar

50g/2oz/¹⁄₃ cup sunflower seeds

25g/1oz/2 tbsp sesame seeds

25g/1oz/¹⁄₄ cup pumpkin seeds

75g/3oz/scant 1 cup rolled oats

75g/3oz/²⁄₃ cup self-raising (self-rising)
 wholemeal (whole-wheat) flour

50g/2oz/²⁄₃ cup desiccated (dry
 unsweetened shredded) coconut

2 eggs

1 Preheat the oven to 200°C/400°F/Gas 6. Grease a 20cm/8in square shallow baking tin (pan) and line with baking parchment.

2 Put the apple sauce in a large bowl with the apricots, raisins, sugar and the sunflower, sesame and pumpkin seeds and stir together with a wooden spoon until thoroughly mixed.

3 Add the oats, flour, coconut and eggs to the fruit mixture and gently stir together until evenly combined.

4 Turn the mixture into the tin and spread to the edges in an even layer. Bake for about 25 minutes or until golden and just firm to the touch.

5 Leave to cool in the tin, then lift out on to a board and cut into bars.

Nutritional information per cookie: Energy 207kcal/871kJ; Protein 4.9g; Carbohydrate 29.3g, of which sugars 19.2g; Fat 8.7g, of which saturates 3g; Cholesterol 32mg; Calcium 65mg; Fibre 2.8g; Sodium 24mg.

Date slice

Lemon-flavoured icing tops these scrumptious, low-fat bars, which are full of succulent fruit and crunchy seeds – the perfect mid-morning pick-me-up with a cup of tea or coffee.

MAKES 12–16

175g/6oz/³/₄ cup light muscovado (brown) sugar

175g/6oz/1 cup ready-to-eat dried dates, chopped

115g/4oz/1 cup self-raising (self-rising) flour

50g/2oz/¹/₂ cup muesli (granola)

30ml/2 tbsp sunflower seeds

15ml/1 tbsp poppy seeds

30ml/2 tbsp sultanas (golden raisins)

150ml/¹/₄ pint/²/₃ cup natural (plain) low-fat yogurt

1 egg, beaten

200g/7oz/1³/₄ cups icing (confectioners') sugar, sifted

lemon juice

15–30ml/1–2 tbsp pumpkin seeds

1 Preheat the oven to 180°C/ 350°F/Gas 4. Line a 28 x 18cm/ 11 x 7in shallow baking tin (pan) with baking parchment. Mix together all the ingredients, except the icing sugar, lemon juice and pumpkin seeds.

2 Spread in the tin and bake for about 25 minutes until golden brown. Leave to cool.

3 To make the topping, put the sifted icing sugar in a small bowl and stir in just enough lemon juice to make a spreading consistency.

4 Spread the icing over the baked date mixture and sprinkle generously with pumpkin seeds. Leave the date slices to harden and set before cutting into squares or bars and serving.

Nutritional information per cookie: Energy 211kcal/893kJ; Protein 3.6g; Carbohydrate 43.6g, of which sugars 35.5g; Fat 3.6g, of which saturates 0.5g; Cholesterol 12mg; Calcium 56mg; Fibre 1.3g; Sodium 18mg.

Spicy fruit slice

A double-layered sweet cookie in which the topping combines dried fruit with grated carrot to keep it moist. An indulgent teatime treat.

MAKES 12–16

90g/3¹/₂oz/7 tbsp vegetable margarine
75g/3oz/¹/₂ cup caster (superfine) sugar
1 egg yolk
115g/4oz/1 cup plain (all-purpose) flour
30ml/2 tbsp self-raising (self-rising) flour
30ml/2 tbsp desiccated (dry
    unsweetened shredded) coconut
icing (confectioners') sugar, for dusting

FOR THE TOPPING
30ml/2 tbsp dried prunes, chopped
30ml/2 tbsp sultanas (golden raisins)
50g/2oz/¹/₂ cup dried pears, chopped
25g/1oz/¹/₄ cup walnuts, chopped
75g/3oz/²/₃ cup self-raising
    (self-rising) flour
5ml/1 tsp ground cinnamon
2.5ml/¹/₂ tsp ground ginger
175g/6oz/generous 1 cup
    grated carrots
1 egg, beaten
75ml/5 tbsp vegetable oil
2.5ml/¹/₂ tsp bicarbonate of soda
    (baking soda)
90g/3¹/₂oz/scant ¹/₂ cup dark
    muscovado (molasses) sugar

1 Preheat the oven to 180°C/350°F/Gas 4. Then line a 28 x 18cm/11 x 7in shallow baking tin (pan) with baking parchment.

2 In a large mixing bowl beat together the margarine, sugar and egg yolk until smooth and creamy.

3 Stir in the plain flour, self-raising flour and coconut and mix together well. Press into the base of the prepared tin, using your fingers to spread the dough evenly.

4 Bake for about 15 minutes, or until firm and light brown.

5 To make the topping, mix together all the ingredients and spread over the cooked base. Bake for about 35 minutes, or until firm. Cool completely in the tin before cutting into bars or squares. Dust with icing sugar.

Nutritional information per cookie: Energy 228kcal/955kJ; Protein 2.7g; Carbohydrate 29.7g, of which sugars 13.9g; Fat 11.8g, of which saturates 3.8g; Cholesterol 25mg; Calcium 34mg; Fibre 1.1g; Sodium 55mg.

Savoury crackers

Cheese and biscuits is a classic

combination, but there are many other

occasions when a savoury crunch is just

what is needed. This superb collection

of delicious and tasty recipes offers

something for all occasions, from

sophisticated Wheat Thins to rustic

Herby Seeded Oatcakes.

Rye and caraway seed sticks

Wonderful with cocktails or pre-dinner drinks and a great addition to the cheeseboard, these long sticks are made with rye flour and have crunchy caraway seeds inside and out.

MAKES 18–20

90g/3¹/₂oz/³/₄ cup plain
  (all-purpose) flour
75g/3oz/²/₃ cup rye flour
2.5ml/¹/₂ tsp salt
2.5ml/¹/₂ tsp baking powder

90g/3¹/₂oz/7 tbsp unsalted (sweet)
  butter, diced
10ml/2 tsp caraway seeds
60ml/4 tbsp boiling water

1 Preheat the oven to 180°C/350°F/Gas 4. Put the flours, salt and baking powder in a bowl and mix together. Add the butter and rub in until the mixture resembles fine breadcrumbs. Stir in 5ml/1 tsp of the caraway seeds. Add the water and mix well to form a soft dough.

2 Divide the dough into about 18 even pieces and, using your fingers, gently roll each one out to a long thin stick about 25cm/10in long. Do not use any flour when rolling out the sticks unless the mixture is a little too moist and try to make the sticks as uniform as possible.

3 Place the sticks on a non-stick baking sheet. Sprinkle over the remaining caraway seeds, rolling the sticks in any spilled seeds.

4 Bake the sticks in the oven for about 20 minutes until crisp. Remove from the oven and transfer carefully to a wire rack to cool.

Nutritional information per cookie: Energy 64kcal/269kJ; Protein 0.9g; Carbohydrate 6.4g, of which sugars 0.1g; Fat 4.1g, of which saturates 2.4g; Cholesterol 10mg; Calcium 12mg; Fibre 0.6g; Sodium 77mg.

Wheat thins

These classic wheat biscuits are especially delicious with rich-tasting creamy cheeses, and also make a quick snack – simply spread with butter when you are in a hurry.

MAKES 18

175g/6oz/1¹/2 cups fine stoneground
    wholemeal (whole-wheat) flour
pinch of salt
5ml/1 tsp baking powder
50g/2oz/¹/2 cup coarse oatmeal
40g/1¹/2oz/3 tbsp granulated sugar
115g/4oz/¹/2 cup unsalted (sweet)
    butter, chilled and diced

1 Preheat the oven to 190°C/ 375°F/Gas 5. Put all the ingredients into a food processor and process until the mixture starts to clump. Tip out on to a floured surface, gather the dough together with your hands and roll out.

2 Stamp out 18 rounds with a 7.5cm/3in round biscuit (cookie) cutter. Place on an ungreased baking sheet. Bake for 12 minutes until just beginning to colour at the edges. Leave to cool slightly, then transfer to a wire rack to cool completely.

Nutritional information per cookie: Energy 98kcal/408kJ; Protein 1.6g; Carbohydrate 10.6g, of which sugars 2.6g; Fat 5.7g, of which saturates 3.4g; Cholesterol 14mg; Calcium 8mg; Fibre 1.1g; Sodium 73mg.

Herby seeded oatcakes

The addition of thyme and sunflower seeds to this traditional recipe makes these oatcakes an especially good accompaniment to cheese – try them spread with goat's cheese or ripe Brie.

MAKES 32

175g/6oz/1½ cups plain wholemeal (whole-wheat) flour
175g/6oz/1½ cups fine oatmeal
5ml/1 tsp salt
1.5ml/¼ tsp bicarbonate of soda (baking soda)
75g/3oz/6 tbsp white vegetable fat (shortening)
15ml/1 tbsp fresh thyme leaves, chopped
30ml/2 tbsp sunflower seeds
rolled oats, for sprinkling

1 Preheat the oven to 150°C/300°F/Gas 2. Sprinkle two ungreased, non-stick baking sheets with rolled oats and set aside.

2 Put the flour, oatmeal, salt and soda in a bowl and rub in the fat until the mixture resembles fine breadcrumbs. Stir in the thyme.

3 Add just enough cold water (about 90–105ml/6–7 tbsp) to the dry ingredients to mix into a stiff but not sticky dough.

4 Gently knead the dough on a lightly floured surface until smooth, then cut roughly in half and roll out one piece on a lightly floured surface to make a 23–25cm/9–10in round.

5 Sprinkle sunflower seeds over the dough and press them in with the rolling pin. Cut into triangles and arrange on one of the baking sheets. Repeat with the remaining dough. Bake for 45–60 minutes until crisp but not brown. Leave the oatcakes to cool on wire racks.

Nutritional information per cookie: Energy 62kcal/259kJ; Protein 1.6g; Carbohydrate 7.7g, of which sugars 0.2g; Fat 3g, of which saturates 0.9g; Cholesterol 0mg; Calcium 6mg; Fibre 0.9g; Sodium 21mg.

Malted wheat and mixed seed crackers

These large crackers have plenty of crunch and flavour provided by the selection of different seeds that are used. They taste fabulous with robust farmhouse cheeses.

MAKES 12–14

250g/9oz/2¼ cups Granary
   (whole-wheat) or malted wheat flour
2.5ml/½ tsp salt
2.5ml/½ tsp baking powder
115g/4oz/½ cup butter, chilled
   and diced

1 egg, beaten
30ml/2 tbsp milk, plus extra for brushing
15ml/1 tbsp pumpkin seeds
15ml/1 tbsp sunflower seeds
15ml/1 tbsp sesame seeds
2.5ml/½ tsp celery salt

1 Preheat the oven to 180°C/350°F/Gas 4. Put the flour, salt, baking powder and butter in a bowl. Rub together until well combined.

2 Add the egg and milk and mix to a stiff dough. Roll out on a floured surface to about 5mm/¼in thick.

3 Using a pastry brush, brush a little milk over the rolled dough. Sprinkle all the pumpkin, sunflower and sesame seeds over the top in an even layer, then sprinkle the celery salt over the top.

4 Very gently, roll the rolling pin back and forth over the seeds to press them into the dough.

5 Stamp out rounds using a 10cm/4in plain cookie cutter, and place on a non-stick baking sheet, spacing them slightly apart. Alternatively, use a sharp knife to trim off the rough edges of the rolled out dough, then cut the dough into equal-size squares, rectangles or triangles.

6 Bake the crackers for about 15 minutes, or until just beginning to brown. Carefully transfer the crackers to a wire rack to cool completely.

Nutritional information per cookie: Energy 140kcal/586kJ; Protein 3.4g; Carbohydrate 12.1g, of which sugars 0.5g; Fat 9.1g, of which saturates 4.6g; Cholesterol 31mg; Calcium 14mg; Fibre 1.8g; Sodium 126mg.

Polenta chip dippers

These tasty Parmesan-flavoured batons are best served warm from the oven with a spicy, tangy dip. A bowl of Thai chilli dipping sauce or a creamy, chilli-spiked guacamole are perfect.

MAKES ABOUT 80

1.5 litres/2¹/₂ pints/6¹/₄ cups water
10ml/2 tsp salt
375g/13oz/3¹/₄ cups instant polenta
150g/5oz/1¹/₂ cups freshly grated
    Parmesan cheese
90g/3¹/₂oz/scant ¹/₂ cup butter
10ml/2 tsp cracked black pepper
salt
olive oil, for brushing

1 Put the water in a heavy pan and bring to the boil over a high heat. Reduce the heat, add the salt and pour in the polenta in a steady stream, stirring constantly. Cook over a low heat, stirring constantly, for about 5 minutes until the mixture thickens and starts to come away from the sides of the pan.

2 Remove from the heat and add the cheese, butter, pepper and salt to taste. Stir well until the butter has completely melted and the mixture is smooth.

3 Pour on to a smooth surface. Spread the polenta out using a metal spatula to a thickness of 2cm/³/₄in and shape into a rectangle. Leave to cool for at least 30 minutes. Meanwhile preheat the oven to 200°C/400°F/ Gas 6 and lightly oil two or three baking sheets with some olive oil.

4 Cut the polenta slab in half, then carefully cut into even strips using a sharp knife. Bake the polenta chips for about 40–50 minutes until they are dark golden brown and crunchy. Turn them over from time to time during cooking. Serve warm.

Nutritional information per cookie: Energy 34kcal/142kJ; Protein 1.2g; Carbohydrate 3.4g, of which sugars 0g; Fat 1.7g, of which saturates 1g; Cholesterol 4mg; Calcium 23mg; Fibre 0.1g; Sodium 27mg.

Herb and garlic twists

These twists are very short and crumbly, made with garlic-flavoured dough sandwiched with fresh herbs and some chilli flakes for an extra kick. A very popular party nibble.

MAKES ABOUT 20

90g/3¹/₂oz/scant ¹/₂ cup butter, at room
   temperature, diced
2 large garlic cloves, crushed
1 egg
1 egg yolk
175g/6oz/1¹/₂ cups self-raising
   (self-rising) flour
large pinch of salt
30ml/2 tbsp chopped fresh mixed
   herbs, such as basil, thyme,
   marjoram and flat
   leaf parsley
2.5–5ml/¹/₂–1 tsp dried chilli flakes
paprika or cayenne pepper,
   for sprinkling

1 Preheat the oven to 200°C/400°F/Gas 6. Put the butter and garlic into a bowl and beat well. Add the egg and yolk and beat in thoroughly. Stir in the flour and salt and mix to a soft but not sticky dough.

2 Roll the dough out on a sheet of baking parchment to a 28cm/11in square. Using a sharp knife, cut it in half to make two rectangles.

3 Sprinkle the herbs and chilli flakes over one of the rectangles, then place the other rectangle on top. Gently roll the rolling pin over the herbs and chilli flakes to press them into the dough.

4 Using a sharp knife, cut the dough into 1cm/¹/₂in sticks. Make two twists in the centre of each one and place on a non-stick baking sheet.

5 Bake for 15 minutes, or until crisp and golden brown. Leave on the baking sheet to cool slightly, then transfer to a wire rack to cool completely. To serve, sprinkle with a little paprika or cayenne pepper, according to taste.

Nutritional information per cookie: Energy 71kcal/295kJ; Protein 1.4g; Carbohydrate 6.9g, of which sugars 0.2g; Fat 4.4g, of which saturates 2.5g; Cholesterol 29mg; Calcium 19mg; Fibre 0.3g; Sodium 32mg.

Poppy seed and sea salt crackers

These attractive little crackers are ideal to use as the base of drinks party canapés, or they can be served plain as tasty nibbles in their own right.

MAKES 20

115g/4oz/1 cup plain (all-purpose) flour
1.5ml/½ tsp salt
5ml/1 tsp caster (superfine) sugar
15g/½oz/1 tbsp butter
15ml/1 tbsp poppy seeds
about 90ml/6 tbsp single (light) cream

FOR THE TOPPING
a little milk
sea salt flakes

1 Preheat the oven to 150°C/300°F/Gas 2. Put the flour, salt and sugar in a bowl and rub in the butter. Stir in the poppy seeds. Add enough cream to mix to a stiff dough. Roll out on a lightly floured surface to a 20 x 25cm/8 x 10in rectangle. Cut into 20 squares.

2 Place the dough squares on an ungreased baking sheet and brush sparingly with milk. Sprinkle a few sea salt flakes over each cracker.

3 Bake in the oven for 30 minutes until crisp but still pale. Transfer to a wire rack to cool.

VARIATION
You can use black or white poppy seeds – or a mixture of the two – for these crackers, or substitute sesame, caraway or celery seeds, if you like.

Nutritional information per cookie: Energy 39kcal/164kJ; Protein 0.8g; Carbohydrate 4.8g, of which sugars 0.4g; Fat 2g, of which saturates 1g; Cholesterol 4mg; Calcium 17mg; Fibre 0.2g; Sodium 6mg.

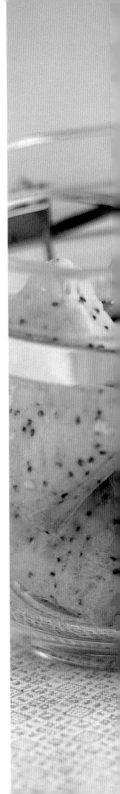

Three-cheese crumble cookies

A delicious combination of mozzarella, Red Leicester and Parmesan cheese and the fresh taste of pesto make these cookies totally irresistible. Make mini ones to serve with drinks.

MAKES 10

225g/8oz/2 cups self-raising
   (self-rising) flour
50g/2oz/¼ cup butter, diced
50g/2oz mozzarella cheese, diced
50g/2oz Red Leicester cheese, diced
15ml/1 tbsp fresh pesto
1 egg
60ml/4 tbsp milk
15g/½oz/2 tbsp grated
   Parmesan cheese
15ml/1 tbsp mixed chopped nuts

1 Preheat the oven to 200°C/400°F/Gas 6. Put the flour in a bowl and rub in the butter until the mixture resembles fine breadcrumbs.

2 Add the diced mozzarella and Red Leicester cheeses to the bowl and stir to mix well. In a separate bowl, beat together the pesto, egg and milk, then pour into the flour and cheese mixture. Stir together quickly until well combined.

3 Using a tablespoon, place in rocky piles on non-stick baking sheets. Sprinkle over the Parmesan cheese and chopped nuts. Bake for 12–15 minutes until well risen and golden brown. Transfer to a wire rack to cool.

Nutritional information per cookie: Energy 182kcal/760kJ; Protein 6.6g; Carbohydrate 17.9g, of which sugars 0.7g; Fat 9.7g, of which saturates 5.3g; Cholesterol 41mg; Calcium 135mg; Fibre 0.8g; Sodium 129mg.

Fennel and chilli ring cookies

Based on an Italian recipe, these cookies are made with yeast and are dry and crumbly. Try them with drinks, dips or with antipasti.

MAKES ABOUT 30

500g/1lb 2oz/4½ cups strong white
   bread flour
115g/4oz/½ cup white vegetable fat
5ml/1 tsp easy-blend (rapid-rise) yeast
15ml/1 tbsp fennel seeds
10ml/2 tsp crushed chilli flakes
15ml/1 tbsp olive oil
400–550ml/14–18fl oz/1⅔–2½ cups
   lukewarm water
olive oil, for brushing

1 Put the flour in a bowl and rub in the fat until the mixture resembles fine breadcrumbs. Add the yeast, fennel and chilli and mix well. Add the oil and enough water to make a soft but not sticky dough. Turn out on to a floured surface and knead lightly.

2 Take small pieces of dough and shape into sausages about 15cm/6in long. Shape into rings and pinch the ends together.

3 Place the rings on a non-stick baking sheet and brush lightly with olive oil. Cover with a dishtowel and set aside for 1 hour to rise slightly.

4 Meanwhile, preheat the oven to 150°C/300°F/Gas 2. Bake the cookies for 1 hour until they are dry and only slightly browned. Leave on the baking sheet to cool completely.

Nutritional information per cookie: Energy 92kcal/385kJ; Protein 1.6g; Carbohydrate 13g, of which sugars 0.3g; Fat 4.1g, of which saturates 1.5g; Cholesterol 1mg; Calcium 24mg; Fibre 0.5g; Sodium 31mg.

Walnut biscotti

These light crunchy cookies with toasted walnuts are flavoured with orange and coriander seeds. The name comes from the Italian word biscotto, meaning twice-baked.

MAKES ABOUT 60

115g/4oz/$\frac{1}{2}$ cup unsalted (sweet)
   butter, diced
200g/7oz/1 cup granulated sugar
2 eggs
15ml/1 tbsp walnut or olive oil
finely grated rind of 1 large orange
350g/12oz/3 cups plain
   (all-purpose) flour
7.5ml/1$\frac{1}{2}$ tsp baking powder
75g/3oz/$\frac{3}{4}$ cup cornmeal
115g/4oz/1 cup toasted
   walnuts, chopped
10ml/2 tsp coriander seeds, crushed

1 Preheat the oven to160°C/325°F/ Gas 3. Put the butter and sugar into a bowl and beat together well. Add the eggs, walnut or olive oil and orange rind and mix well.

2 Sift the flour and baking powder over the mixture and add the cornmeal, walnuts and coriander seeds. Then mix thoroughly and bring together to form a soft but not sticky dough.

3 Shape the dough into four equal-sized logs, about 18cm/7in long and 5cm/2in in diameter. Place slightly apart on non-stick baking sheets. Bake for 35 minutes until they are lightly golden.

4 Leave the logs to cool for 10 minutes on wire racks, then slice diagonally into 1cm/$\frac{1}{2}$in slices. Place on the baking sheets and bake for a further 10 minutes.

Nutritional information per cookie: Energy 69kcal/289kJ; Protein 1.2g; Carbohydrate 9g, of which sugars 3.6g; Fat 5g, of which saturates 1.2g; Cholesterol 11mg; Calcium 13mg; Fibre 0.3g; Sodium 15mg.

Parmesan tuiles

These lacy tuiles look very impressive, but they couldn't be easier to make. Believe or not, they use only a single ingredient – Parmesan cheese.

MAKES 8–10

115g/4oz Parmesan cheese

1 Preheat the oven to 200°C/ 400°F/Gas 6. Line two baking sheets with baking parchment. Grate the cheese using a fine grater, pulling it down slowly to make long strands.

2 Spread the grated cheese out in 7.5–9cm/3–3¹⁄₂in rounds. Do not spread the cheese too thickly; it should just cover the parchment.

3 Bake the tuiles for 5–7 minutes until bubbling and golden brown.

4 Leave the tuiles on the baking sheet for about 30 seconds and then carefully transfer, using a metal spatula, to a wire rack to cool completely. Alternatively, drape over a rolling pin to make a curved shape.

Nutritional information per cookie: Energy 52kcal/216kJ; Protein 4.5g; Carbohydrate 0g, of which sugars 0g; Fat 3.8g, of which saturates 2.4g; Cholesterol 12mg; Calcium 138mg; Fibre 0g; Sodium 125mg.

The art of making and baking cookies

Cookies are simple to make but there

is some basic know-how that will

make the process even easier.

This chapter explains everything you

will ever need – from basic equipment

and ingredients to making and baking

different types of cookies, as well as

decorating and storing them.

Cookie ingredients

Most cookies are made from a few basic ingredients – butter, sugar, flour and sometimes eggs and other ingredients and flavourings. To ensure you make the best cookies, always try to use really fresh, good quality ingredients.

BUTTER

Unsalted (sweet) butter is best for making cookies; it has a sweet, slightly nutty taste and a firm texture, which is particularly well-suited to cookies made using the rubbed-in method.

The temperature of butter is important. For rubbed-in cookies butter should be cold and firm but not too hard; take it out of the refrigerator 5 minutes before using. To cream butter, it should be at room temperature. This is very important if you are beating by hand. If you forget to take butter out of the

ABOVE: *White vegetable fat (left) and block margarine (right) work well in some cookie recipes.*

refrigerator in advance, soften it in the microwave on low power for 10–15 seconds.

If you need to melt butter, dice it so that it melts more quickly and evenly. Melt over a very low heat to prevent it burning and remove from the heat when it has almost melted; the residual heat will complete the job. If you need to brush baking tins (pans) or sheets with melted butter, use unsalted butter rather than salted, which tends to burn and stick.

Storing butter

Butter should be stored in the refrigerator or freezer. It absorbs flavours easily so protect it from strong ingredients by wrapping in baking parchment or foil. If possible, store in a separate compartment.

Salted butter can be stored in the refrigerator for about a month but unsalted butter should be used within 2 weeks. Alternatively, you can store unsalted butter in the freezer and transfer it to the refrigerator 1–2 days before you need it. All butter can be frozen for up to 6 months.

ABOVE: *Unsalted butter produces cookies with a wonderfully rich flavour and warm golden colour.*

OTHER FATS

Margarine This won't produce the same flavour as butter but it is usually less expensive and can be used in the same way. Block margarines are better for cookie-making, although soft margarine may be used for creaming.

White cooking fats Made from blended vegetable oils or a mixture of vegetable and animal or fish oils, white fats are flavourless and create light, short-textured cookies. They work well in highly flavoured cookies, in which you wouldn't taste the butter. Lard is an opaque white fat made from rendered pork fat and features in some traditional cookie recipes.

Oil This may sometimes be used instead of solid fat. Sunflower and safflower oils are preferable as they have a mild taste. Olive oil has a distinctive flavour but may be added to savoury crackers.

SUGAR

There are many different types of sugar, all of which add their own distinctive character to cookies.

Refined sugars

Produced from sugar cane and sugar beet, refined white sugar is 99.9 per cent pure sucrose.

Granulated/white sugar This has large granules and can be used in rubbed-in mixtures or to make a crunchy cookie topping.

Caster/superfine sugar This is the most frequently used sugar for cookie-making. It has a fine grain so is ideal for creaming with butter. It is also used for melted mixtures, meringue toppings and sprinkling over freshly baked cookies.

Icing/confectioners' sugar This fine, powdery sugar is used to make smooth icings and fillings and for dusting over cookies after baking. It may also be added to some piped mixtures.

Soft brown sugar This is refined white sugar that has been tossed in molasses or syrup to colour and flavour it; the darker the colour, the more

RIGHT: (Left to right) Soft brown sugar and demerara (raw) sugar give cookies a slightly caramel taste.

intense the flavour. It makes moister cookies than white sugar, so never substitute one for the other.

Unrefined sugars

Derived from raw sugar cane, these retain some molasses. They often have a more intense flavour but tend to be less sweet than refined sugars.

Golden caster/superfine sugar and granulated sugar These are pale gold and are used in the same way as their white counterparts.

Demerara (raw) sugar This rich golden sugar has a slight toffee flavour. The grains are large; it is only used in cookie doughs if a crunchy texture is required. It is good for sprinkling over cookies before baking.

Muscovado/molasses sugar This fine-textured, moist soft brown sugar has a treacly flavour.

Storing sugar

Sugar should always be stored in an airtight container. If white sugar forms clumps, break it up

ABOVE: Coarse-grained granular sugar is good for sprinkling.

LEFT: Fine-grained caster sugar is widely used in cookie doughs.

with your fingers. If brown sugar dries out and hardens, soften it by warming it in the microwave for about 1 minute. Alternatively, place it in a bowl and cover with a damp cloth for about 1 hour. The sugar absorbs the moisture from the cloth.

OTHER SWEETENERS

There are many other ingredients that can be used as sweeteners besides sugar.

Golden/light corn syrup Slightly less sweet than sugar, this produces moist, sticky cookies and is often used in no-bake recipes.

Maple syrup Thinner than golden syrup, maple syrup has a very distinctive flavour.

Honey Use blended honey in cookie doughs as the flavour of milder honeys will be lost.

Malt extract This concentrated extract made from barley has a distinctive flavour, thick consistency and dark, almost black colour.

Molasses A by-product of sugar refining, molasses looks like malt extract but has a slightly bitter taste.

FLOUR

Most cookie recipes use plain (all-purpose) flour as it has a low gluten content, resulting in a crumbly texture. The grains are processed then treated with chlorine to make the flour whiter. You can also buy unbleached flour, which has a greyish colour. Some flour is pre-sifted but you should sift it anyway as the contents tend to settle during storage. Flour, even the same type and brand, may vary slightly, so always hold a few drops of liquid back in case they aren't needed.

ABOVE: *Wholemeal (whole-wheat) flour gives cookies a lovely taste.*

Self-raising flour

Known as self-rising flour in the United States, this flour contains raising agents that make cookies spread and rise, giving them a lighter texture. If you run out of self-raising flour, you can substitute plain flour, adding 5ml/1 tsp baking powder to each 115g/4oz/1 cup. Self-raising flour should not be kept for longer than 3 months because raising agents gradually deteriorate.

Wholemeal flour

Also known as whole-wheat flour, this is milled from the entire wheat kernel and contains all the nutrients and flavour of wheat. It is coarser than white flour, giving a heavier result. It absorbs more liquid than white flour so recipes should be adjusted if wholemeal flour is used.

Brown (wheatmeal) flour, contains less of the bran and wheat germ – only 80–90 per cent. This means it has a much finer texture and milder taste than wholemeal flour.

ABOVE: *Rice flour is often added to shortbread to give a crumbly texture.*

LEFT: *Cornmeal produces cookies with a golden colour, delicious flavour and distinctive texture.*

Non-wheat flours

These can be great for cookie making, although some should be combined with wheat flour.

Potato flour This fine powder is made from potato starch and can be mixed with wheat flour to give a lighter texture to cookies.

Chestnut flour This light brown, nutty-flavoured flour is made from ground chestnuts and is often sold in Italian delicatessens.

Cornmeal Also known as polenta or maizemeal, this is bright yellow and coarse or medium ground.

Cornflour/cornstarch This fine white powder is made from the middle of the maize kernel. It is often used in piped cookie mixtures to give a smooth texture.

Soya flour Made from soya beans, this has a distinctive nutty flavour. It has a high protein content. Medium- and low-fat varieties are available.

Rice flour This is made by finely grinding polished white rice and is used in many cookie recipes, to give a short, slightly crumbly texture.

Gluten-free baking

Some people are allergic or intolerant to the protein gluten, which is found in both wheat and rye. Specially produced gluten-free and wheat-free flour mixtures can be used for baking, as can any of the naturally gluten-free flours such as cornmeal, potato flour, rice flour and soya flour.

ABOVE:
*Bicarbonate of
soda (baking
soda) and baking
powder give cookies
a lighter texture.*

RAISING AGENTS

Although cookies are usually made
with plain (all-purpose) flour, raising
agents may be added to give them a
lighter texture. Raising agents make
cookies spread more, so space them
well apart for baking.

Raising agents react when they come
in contact with water and produce
carbon dioxide bubbles that make the
cookie rise during baking. Cookie
doughs containing raising agents must
therefore be shaped and baked as soon
as liquid is added. Store raising agents
in a dry place and use within their use-
by date as they deteriorate with age,
becoming less effective.

Baking powder This is a mixture
of alkaline bicarbonate of soda
(baking soda) and an acid such as
cream of tartar.

Bicarbonate of soda/baking
soda This can be added to a cookie
mixture that contains any type of
acidic ingredient.

RIGHT: *Eggs are widely used in cookie-
making and can help to produce rich,
golden cookies with a great flavour.*

EGGS

These are used to enrich cookie
doughs and bind dry ingredients. They
are often included in rolled doughs
because they prevent the mixture
from spreading too much during
baking. If a recipe does not specify the
size of an egg, use a medium (US
large) one.

For baking, eggs should be at room
temperature; cold egg yolks may
curdle and cold egg whites will
produce less volume when whisked.
Add eggs to a creamed mixture a
little at a time, beating after each
addition and adding 15ml/1 tbsp
sifted flour if the mixture starts to
curdle. Whisk egg whites in a very
clean bowl and use straight away.

Buying and storing eggs

Always check the use-by date on eggs
and never buy cracked, damaged or
dirty eggs. A fresh egg will have a
round, plump yolk and a thick white
that clings closely to the yolk. Store
eggs in the refrigerator, pointed-end
down. Do not store near strong-
smelling foods or possible
contaminants such as raw meat; their
shells are porous and can absorb
odours and bacteria.

Separating eggs

Some recipes require only an
egg yolk or an egg white. Egg-
separating devices are available from
kitchenware stores but it is easy to
separate eggs by hand.

1 Tap the middle of the egg sharply
against the rim of a bowl, then,
holding the egg over the bowl,
prise the shell apart with the tips of
your thumbs.

2 Gently tip the white into the
bowl, retaining the yolk in the shell.
Tip the yolk into the other half-shell,
letting any remaining white fall into
the bowl.

COOK'S TIP

*You can also separate the yolk of an
egg from the white by breaking the egg and
tipping the whole egg into the palm of your
hand and letting the white slowly drain into
a bowl through your fingers.*

FRUIT, NUTS AND SEEDS

Dried, candied and crystallized fruit, nuts and seeds can be added to cookie doughs to add flavour, colour and texture, or to decorate.

Dried fruit

The drying process intensifies the flavour and sweetness of the fruit.
Vine fruit These include sultanas (golden raisins), raisins and currants. Buy seedless fruit, choosing a reliable brand or go for fruit in clear bags so that you can check its softness and colour. It can be kept in an airtight container for up to a year, but is best used within 6 months.
Apricots These are produced in California and other parts of the American Pacific coast, Australia, South Africa, Turkey and Iran. Some are very dry and need to be soaked in liquid before using; others, labelled ready-to-eat, have a soft texture and are better for cookie-making.
Apples and pears Dried in rings or as halved fruit, they are best used finely chopped and added to drop cookie mixtures.

Tropical fruits Exotic fruits such as papaya and mango are available dried and have an intense flavour and vibrant colour.
Cranberries and sour cherries These are brightly coloured and add a wonderful sweet-and-sour flavour to cookies.
Candied and crystallized fruits Fresh fruits such as whole pitted cherries and apricots or pieces of pineapple and angelica are steeped in sugar and are usually used to decorate cookies.

Nuts

These can be added to cookie mixtures or chopped and sprinkled over unbaked cookies. Always buy fresh nuts in small quantities, then chop as necessary. Store in an airtight container, ideally in the refrigerator or freezer.
Almonds Sweet almonds are available ready-blanched, chopped, split, flaked (sliced) and ground.
Brazil nuts These wedge-shaped nuts are actually a seed. Their creamy white flesh has a sweet milky taste and a high fat content. Store carefully and use within a few months.
Cashew nuts These kidney-shaped nuts are always sold shelled and dried. They have a sweet flavour and almost crumbly texture.
Coconut White, dense coconut flesh is made into desiccated (dry unsweetened shredded) coconut and flakes.

LEFT: *Dried fruit such as apricots and pears make a delicious, healthy addition to cookies.*

ABOVE: *Hazelnuts have a lovely nutty taste and can be used whole or chopped into small pieces.*

Hazelnuts These are very good chopped and toasted, as this brings out their flavour.
Macadamia nuts These round, white, buttery nuts are native to Australia but are now also grown in California and South America.
Peanuts Strictly speaking, these are a legume not a nut, as they grow underground. Peanuts may be used raw or roasted, but do not use salted nuts unless specified.
Pecan nuts These are rather like elongated walnuts in appearance, but with a milder, sweeter flavour.
Pine nuts These are small and creamy coloured, and have an almost oily texture and aromatic flavour.
Pistachio nuts Bright green, these are often used for decorating cookies.
Walnuts These are well flavoured with a crunchy texture.

Seeds

These are a popular ingredient in wholesome cookies and savoury crackers. They can be added to cookie doughs to give a crunchy texture or sprinkled over the tops of cookies before they are baked to give an attractive finish.

FLAVOURINGS

There are many flavourings that can be added to cookies. These can include the less obvious flavours of grated lemon, lime or orange rind, the juice of citrus fruits, rose water, orange flower water and almond extract. Flavourings may add a subtle or strong taste, and some can also add texture.

Chocolate

From cocoa-flavoured drop cookies to chocolate chip and chocolate-coated varieties, chocolate is the most popular cookie flavouring.

Dark/bittersweet chocolate This has a bitter flavour and is the most popular chocolate for cookie-making.

Plain (semisweet) chocolate This contains at least 50 per cent cocoa solids; the eating variety may contain as little as 25 per cent. It can be added to cookie doughs, but does not melt well.

Milk chocolate This contains milk powder and a higher percentage of sugar than plain chocolate. It is more difficult to melt.

White chocolate This contains no cocoa solids, only cocoa butter, milk solids and sugar. Brands that contain more cocoa butter are best for baking and melting.

Couverture This fine-quality plain, milk or white chocolate can be bought from specialist stores and by mail order. It melts beautifully and makes glossy cookie coatings.

Chocolate chips or dots These tiny chocolate pieces melt well and are easy to work with. The milk and white versions are more stable than bars of milk and white chocolate.

Chocolate cake covering This usually contains little real chocolate and is flavoured with cocoa powder. It melts well and is good for coating cookies, but has a poor flavour.

Unsweetened cocoa powder This bitter, dark powder can be added to cookie mixtures or dusted over the tops of cookies.

Storing chocolate Chocolate should always be wrapped in foil and kept in a dry, cool place. In hot weather, it can be kept in the refrigerator.

Spices and herbs

Adding spices to cookies is a great way to add flavour. Warm spices such as cinnamon, ginger and nutmeg are mainly used in sweet cookies, while whole spice seeds such as cumin and fennel and ground ones such as coriander are great in crackers.

Vanilla is perhaps the spice most frequently added to sweet cookies, providing a fragrant, delicate flavour. Vanilla sugar is one of the easiest ways to add the flavouring. Pure vanilla extract, which is distilled from vanilla pods (beans), is also a good way to add the flavour.

Fresh or dried herbs can be added to savoury cookie doughs or sprinkled on top before baking.

Alcohol

Spirits, sherry and liqueurs can be added to cookie mixtures instead of liquid such as milk. During baking the alcohol will evaporate, leaving a subtle flavour.

Salt

This helps to bring out the flavour in both sweet cookies and crackers, but add only the tiniest pinch, especially if using salted butter. Coarse crystals of sea salt can be used to sprinkle over savoury cookies to decorate.

BELOW: *Chocolate – in its many forms – is a classic cookie ingredient.*

Equipment

Most cookies can be made with just weighing scales or calibrated measuring cups, a mixing bowl, fine sieve, rolling pin, wooden spoon, baking sheet and a wire rack. However, there are a few pieces of equipment that can make cookie-making even easier. These include electrical gadgets, piping bags and cookie presses.

BOWLS
Large bowls are good for mixing doughs, while medium and small heatproof bowls are good for melting butter or chocolate and beating eggs.

ELECTRICAL APPLIANCES
Food mixers and processors are great for creaming together butter and sugar and for beating in eggs. A hand-held electric whisk can be used for beating eggs, whisking egg whites and beating together butter and sugar and it has the advantage that it can be used in a pan over heat.

MEASURING SPOONS, CUPS AND JUGS
A set of accurate measuring spoons is essential. Ordinary spoons vary in size so invest in a commercially produced set. For measuring larger volumes of dry ingredients and liquids, you will need a clearly calibrated measuring jug (cup).

SIEVES
You should invest in a set of strong, fine sieves in at least two sizes; a large one for sifting dry ingredients such as flour, and a smaller one for dusting icing (confectioners') sugar or unsweetened cocoa powder over baked cookies.

PALETTE KNIVES AND METAL SPATULAS
Wide and round-bladed palette knives and metal spatulas are essential for

ABOVE: *A set of special measuring spoons and jugs or measuring cups are essential for successful cookie-making.*

BELOW: *A set of heatproof bowls for mixing, and beating ingredients is invaluable.*

lifting cookies from baking sheets and can also be used for mixing liquid into cookie doughs and mixtures. Small ones are very useful for spreading cookie fillings and icing on to cookies.

WHISKS
A wire balloon whisk or hand-held rotary whisk are useful for whisking egg whites for cookies such as macaroons and for whipping cream to use in fillings. They are also good for removing lumps in icing.

ABOVE: *The flexible wires of a balloon whisk will incorporate air into everything from eggs to cream.*

LEFT: *An electric food mixer takes the hard work out of cookie-making and can be a real time saver.*

ROLLING PINS

These come in all shapes and sizes, some with handles and some without.

BAKING SHEETS

These are either entirely flat or have a lip along the length of one side; baking trays have a lip all around the edges. Baking sheets are preferable as they allow better air movement around the cookies, but be careful when removing cookies from the oven because they can slip off easily.

TINS/PANS

These are available in many shapes and sizes from round, square and rectangular to petal-shaped. They are used for baking cookie doughs such as shortbread and also for bar and brownie mixtures.

WIRE RACKS

After baking, most cookies should be transferred to a wire rack to cool. The rack allows air to circulate, preventing trapped warmth turning into moisture and making the cookies soggy. Some cookies should be left on the baking sheet for a few minutes to firm up before transferring to a wire rack.

TIMERS

These are absolutely essential for baking. Even an extra 1 or 2 minutes in the oven can result in overbaked or burnt cookies. Many modern ovens are fitted with a timer, but if you do not have an oven with a timer, it is worth investing in a separate timer.

COOKIE CUTTERS

These come in many different shapes and sizes from the simplest plain or fluted round cutters to people-, animal- and heart-shaped ones.

COOKIE PRESSES

Soft cookie dough can be shaped using a cookie press. The presses look like an icing syringe and work in a similar way. The dough is forced through a disc, which shapes the dough into a pretty cookie.

ABOVE: *Metal cutters are better for cookie-making than plastic ones, which can compress the cut edges.*

ABOVE: *A pastry brush is very useful for brushing unbaked cookies with a milk or beaten egg glaze.*

PIPING/PASTRY BAGS AND NOZZLES

A medium to large piping bag and a selection of both plain and fluted nozzles is useful for piping uncooked cookie dough. Smaller piping bags are extremely good for decorating baked cookies with icing or buttercream.

PASTRY BRUSHES

These brushes are used for glazing unbaked cookies with milk or beaten egg, or baked cookies with a thin sugar glaze.

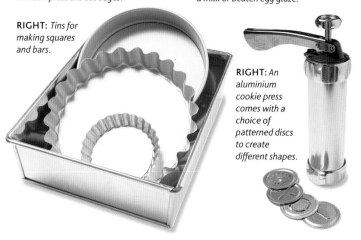

RIGHT: *Tins for making squares and bars.*

RIGHT: *An aluminium cookie press comes with a choice of patterned discs to create different shapes.*

Methods of making cookies

There are many different ways of making cookie dough. Depending on the type of cookie you are baking, the method will vary, so it is extremely useful to know all the techniques.

THE CREAMING METHOD

A wide variety of cookies are made using the creaming method. These include plain Shrewsbury cookies, French sablés, fork cookies, Swiss butter cookies and melting moments. The fat and sugar are creamed – or beaten – together either until just blended or, more usually, until they are well-aerated and have a light and fluffy texture. Eggs and dry ingredients are then added a little bit at a time.

The fat should be soft enough to beat easily, so remember to remove it from the refrigerator at least 30 minutes before you plan to start cookie-making. Unsalted (sweet) butter is the best choice, but if you are going to use margarine, use the firm block type rather than softer margarine that is sold in tubs.

The eggs should also be at room temperature or they may curdle the creamed mixture when they are added. It is not essential to use an electric mixer or food processor for the creaming method – a wooden spoon does a perfectly good job – but it definitely makes the process easier and quicker.

Swiss butter cookies

These crisp cookies are very easy to make and delicious to eat.

MAKES 24

115g/4oz/¹/2 cup unsalted (sweet) butter, softened
50g/2oz/¹/4 cup caster (superfine) sugar
1 egg
200g/7oz/1³/4 cups plain (all-purpose) flour
30ml/2 tbsp cornflour (cornstarch)
15ml/1 tbsp ground almonds

1 Put the butter in a large mixing bowl and beat with an electric mixer or a wooden spoon until it is softened and creamy. Add the sugar and beat in until it is incorporated. Continue beating until the mixture is light, fluffy and much paler in colour.

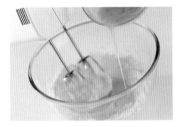

2 Carefully break the egg into a small bowl and beat lightly with a fork. Add the egg to the mixture, a little at a time, making sure to beat well with the mixer after each addition.

3 Sift the flour and cornflour over the creamed ingredients. This will remove any lumps and incorporate air, making your cookies lighter. Add the ground almonds and stir together to make a soft dough.

4 Shape the dough into a ball, then flatten it slightly into a round. Wrap the dough tightly in clear film (plastic wrap) and chill for about 30 minutes, or until the dough is firm. Meanwhile, preheat the oven to 180°C/350°F/Gas 4. Lightly grease two baking sheets or line them with baking parchment.

5 Roll out the dough on a lightly floured surface to 3mm/¹/8in thick. Cut the dough into rounds with a 7.5cm/3in plain cutter and place on the baking sheets. Bake for about 15 minutes until golden. Leave the cookies on the baking sheets for about 5 minutes, then transfer to a wire rack to cool completely.

THE RUBBING-IN METHOD

Many traditional cookies, such as shortbread and digestive biscuits (Graham crackers) are made by rubbing the fat, which can be butter, margarine, white vegetable fat or lard, into the flour.

The fat should be firm and cool but not straight from the refrigerator, so leave the fat at room temperature before using. Beaten eggs, milk or water may also be added to bind the mixture together.

Classic shortbread

These buttery cookies are cooked in a round, then cut into wedges.

MAKES 8 WEDGES

175g/6oz/1¹/₂ cups plain (all-purpose) flour
115g/4oz/¹/₂ cup butter, diced
    and chilled
50g/2oz/¹/₄ cup caster (superfine) sugar,
    plus extra for sprinkling

1 Preheat the oven to 160°C/ 325°F/Gas 3. Then grease a large baking sheet or line it with baking parchment. Sift the flour and salt into a large bowl. Stir in the butter until the pieces are coated with flour. Rub them between your fingertips until the mixture looks like fine breadcrumbs. Next, stir in the sugar.

2 Holding the bowl firmly, gather the dough into a ball. Knead the dough on a lightly floured work surface for about 30 seconds until smooth.

3 Roll out the dough into a round about 15cm/6in in diameter and 1cm/¹/₂in thick. Transfer to the prepared baking sheet. Score the top deeply into eight sections, then prick a pattern with a fork. This will allow steam to escape during cooking and prevent the shortbread from rising in the middle. Chill in the refrigerator for about 1 hour.

4 Sprinkle the top of the shortbread with a little extra caster sugar. Bake in the oven for 35 minutes, or until it is a pale, golden straw colour. Leave to cool on the baking sheet for 5 minutes, then transfer the shortbread on to a wire rack and leave to cool completely before cutting into pieces and serving.

Making rubbed-in cookies in a food processor

This method of making cookies is especially useful where the cookie mixture contains a high proportion of fat.

1 Put the sifted flour and other dry ingredients, such as salt, into the food processor. Process for 4–5 seconds.

2 Sprinkle in the diced, chilled fat. Process for 10 seconds, or until the mixture resembles fine breadcrumbs.

3 Sprinkle any liquid you are using such as beaten egg, milk or water, over the mixture and, using the pulse button, process for just a few seconds until the mixture starts to hold together. Do not allow the cookie dough to form a ball in the food processor.

4 Remove the mixture from the food processor and form into a ball with your hands. Gently knead the dough on a lightly floured work surface for a few seconds until it is smooth.

5 Wrap the dough in clear film (plastic wrap) and then chill in the refrigerator until fairly firm.

THE MELTED METHOD

Cookies such as flapjacks and gingernuts (gingersnaps) are made by first melting the fat and sugar or syrup together. The dry ingredients are then stirred in to make a soft dough that firms as it cools. The baked cookies become crisp as they cool, so should be quickly shaped, or left for a few minutes to firm up before transferring to a wire rack.

Gingernuts

When baked, these spiced cookies are slightly cracked on the top.

MAKES 24

50g/2oz/¹/₄ cup butter, diced
50g/2oz/¹/₄ cup golden (light corn) syrup
40g/1¹/₂oz/3 tbsp granulated (white) sugar
115g/4oz/1 cup self-raising (self-rising) flour
5ml/1 tsp ground ginger
5ml/1 tsp bicarbonate of soda (baking soda)

1 Preheat the oven to 180°C/350°F/ Gas 4. Grease two baking sheets. Put the butter, syrup and sugar in a pan and heat gently until just melted, stirring occasionally until the ingredients are blended. Do not let the mixture boil or some of the liquid will evaporate, altering the proportions.

2 Remove the pan from the heat and leave the mixture to cool for a few minutes.

3 Sift the flour, ginger and bicarbonate of soda over the cookie mixture. Stir until the mixture has blended and is smooth.

4 Place small spoonfuls of the mixture on to the prepared baking sheets, spacing the mounds of cookie dough well apart to allow room for the cookies to spread.

5 Bake the gingernuts in the oven for about 10 minutes, or until they are a light golden brown and the surfaces are crazed.

6 Leave the gingernut cookies on the baking sheets for about 2 minutes to firm up, then carefully transfer them to a wire rack using a metal spatula. Allow to cool and crisp up before serving.

THE ALL-IN-ONE METHOD

Some cookies are made by placing all of the ingredients in a large bowl and beating them together. This method can be made even faster by using a food processor, although chunky ingredients such as dried fruit and nuts may have to be stirred in after mixing the cookie dough. It is essential that the fat is soft enough to blend into the mixture easily.

Raisin cookies

The natural sweetness of raisins gives these cookies extra flavour and bite.

MAKES 24

150g/5oz/1¹/₄ cups plain (all-purpose) flour
2.5ml/¹/₂ tsp baking powder
pinch of salt
115g/4oz/generous ¹/₂ cup caster (superfine) sugar
115g/4oz/¹/₂ cup soft margarine
1 egg, lightly beaten
2.5ml/¹/₂ tsp vanilla extract
150g/5oz/1 cup seedless raisins

1 Preheat the oven to 190°C/375°F/ Gas 5. Lightly grease three baking sheets. Sift the flour, baking powder and salt into a bowl. Add the sugar, margarine, egg and vanilla essence.

2 Beat with a wooden spoon or blend in a food processor until combined. Stir in the raisins.

3 Drop dessertspoonfuls of the mixture about 5cm/2in apart on to the baking sheets. Bake for 15 minutes or until golden brown. Allow to cool a little before transferring to wire racks to cool completely.

THE WHISKED METHOD

Airy cookies or any crisp, delicate cookies, such as tuiles, macaroons and *langues de chat* are made by folding all of the dry ingredients into a whisked mixture of eggs and sugar, or into a meringue (whisked egg whites and sugar) mixture.

Tuiles

These delicate cookies are very popular in France. They are named after the French curved roof tiles, which they closely resemble if they are shaped into curls while still hot.

MAKES 12

1 egg white
50g/2oz/¹/4 cup caster (superfine) sugar
25g/1oz/2 tbsp butter, melted
    and cooled
25g/1oz/¹/4 cup plain (all-purpose)
    flour, sifted
flaked (sliced) almonds, for
    sprinkling (optional)

1 Preheat the oven to 190°C/375°F/ Gas 5. Grease several large baking sheets or line them with baking parchment.

2 Put the egg white in a large, clean, grease-free mixing bowl and, using an electric beater, whisk lightly until stiff peaks form.

3 Gently fold in the caster sugar with a spoon to make a stiff and glossy mixture. (It should resemble a meringue mixture.)

4 Carefully trickle about a third of the melted butter down the side of the bowl and then fold in with the same quantity of flour.

5 Continue doing this until all the butter and flour are incorporated.

6 Place small spoonfuls of the mixture, at least 13cm/5in apart, on the prepared baking sheets, then spread out into thin rounds using the back of a spoon.

7 Sprinkle flaked almonds over each round, if using.

8 Bake the tuiles for 6–7 minutes, or until the biscuits are pale beige in the middle and brown at the edges. Leave to cool on the baking sheets for a few seconds, then lift off carefully with a metal spatula and cool on a wire rack.

9 For really authentic-looking tuiles, make sure to curl them soon after you remove from the oven, while they are still hot.

Measuring different ingredients

Dry ingredients by weight Whether you measure ingredients in imperial or metric, electronic and balance scales will generally give more accurate readings than spring scales. Spoon or pour the dry ingredients into the bowl or tray on the scales and check the reading or dial carefully.

Dry ingredients in measuring cups or spoons To measure a dry ingredient in a spoon, scoop it up in the spoon, then level the surface carefully, using the straight edge of a knife. If you are using measuring cups, make sure you have ¹/4, ¹/3, ¹/2, ²/3, ³/4 and 1 cup sizes. Where a recipe calls for a scant cup, fill the cup with the dry ingredient, level with the back of a knife, then scoop out about 15ml/1 tbsp. Where a generous cup is called for, level with a knife then add about 15ml/1 tbsp.

Liquids in litres, pints or cups Use a clear glass or plastic jug (cup) with calibrations in litres, pints or cups. Put it on to a flat surface, pour in the liquid and carefully check the markings by bending down and looking at eye level.

Liquids in spoons Use proper measuring spoons and carefully pour in the liquid, filling it to the brim before pouring it into the mixing bowl. Do not hold the spoon over the bowl when measuring the liquid or you may end up with a mixture that is too runny.

Drop cookies

These are probably the simplest cookies to make. They are called drop cookies because the dough is soft enough to drop off the spoon and on to the baking sheet. The basic mixture is often made by the creaming method where butter and sugar are beaten together until light and fluffy. Eggs are then beaten in, followed by flour, raising agents and any flavourings.

Chocolate chip cookies

Created in the 1930s, these were originally called Toll House cookies.

MAKES 12

115g/4oz/¹/₂ cup butter, softened

115g/4oz/generous ¹/₂ cup caster (superfine) sugar

1 egg, lightly beaten

5ml/1 tsp vanilla extract

175g/6oz/1¹/₂ cups plain (all-purpose) flour

175g/6oz/1 cup plain (semisweet) chocolate chips

1 Preheat the oven to 180°C/350°F/ Gas 4. Lightly grease several large baking sheets or line them with baking parchment. Cream the butter and sugar together in a bowl until pale and fluffy. Beat in the egg and vanilla extract. Sift the flour over the butter mixture and fold in with the chocolate chips.

2 Carefully drop tablespoonfuls of the cookie mixture on to the prepared baking sheets. Leave plenty of space between the cookies to allow for spreading while baking.

3 Gently flatten each cookie slightly with the back of a fork, trying to keep the shape of each cookie as even as possible.

4 For dropped cookies that have a soft or cakey texture when cooked, the mixture should be left well mounded on the baking sheet and not flattened. Very stiff mixtures should be more widely spread out on the baking sheet. The recipe instructions should indicate this – if you are at all unsure, test how much the mixture spreads by baking a single cookie.

5 Bake the cookies in the oven for about 10 minutes, or until they are a light golden brown colour. Using a metal spatula, carefully transfer to a wire rack to cool completely before serving.

Flavouring drop cookies

As long as you follow the basic recipe, you can make a huge variety of drop cookies. Remember, though, that some added ingredients may alter the consistency of the dough – chopped fresh fruit, for example, may make the mixture too wet, whereas rolled oats will soak up moisture.

Chocolate Substitute 15ml/1 tbsp unsweetened cocoa powder for the same quantity of flour. For a chunkier texture, use coarsely chopped chocolate instead of chocolate chips.
Mocha Use coffee extract instead of vanilla extract.
Macadamia nut or hazelnut Add whole or coarsely chopped nuts

instead of the chocolate chips.
Dried fruit In place of the chocolate chips, add chopped dried fruit, such as raisins, sultanas (golden raisins), apricots, glacé (candied) cherries, or a mixture of candied tropical fruit, such as pineapple, mango and papaya. Add fruit juice or milk instead of vanilla extract.

MELTED DROP COOKIES

Thin, crisp cookies, such as tuiles, florentines and brandy snaps, require the butter and sugar or syrup to be melted together first in order to start the caramelization process prior to baking. Such cookies usually contain little flour, which helps them spread on the baking sheet – so make sure they have plenty of room.

Brandy snaps

These classic melted drop cookies have a wonderful brittle texture. They melt in the mouth to release a sweet, almost caramelized flavour.

MAKES 12–14

75g/3oz/6 tbsp butter, diced
75g/3oz/scant ¹/₂ cup caster
    (superfine) sugar
45ml/3 tbsp golden (light corn) syrup
75g/3oz/²/₃ cup plain
    (all-purpose) flour
5ml/1 tsp ground ginger
30ml/2 tbsp brandy
15ml/1 tbsp lemon juice

1 Preheat the oven to 190°C/375°F/ Gas 5. Lightly grease several baking sheets. Heat the butter, sugar and syrup gently, stirring occasionally until the mixture has melted and becomes smooth.

2 Remove from the heat and leave to cool for a few minutes or the flour will start to cook when it is added.

3 Sift together the flour and ground ginger and stir into the butter mixture with the brandy and lemon juice. Leave for a further 1–2 minutes to allow the flour to absorb some of the moisture.

4 Carefully drop teaspoonfuls of the mixture at 4cm/1¹/₂in intervals on to the prepared baking sheets. Do not attempt to cook any more than three or four on each sheet as they will need room to spread.

5 Bake in the oven, one sheet at a time, for about 8–10 minutes, or until the cookies turn bubbly, lacy in texture and golden brown. Remove the brandy snaps from the oven and leave for about 15 seconds to firm up slightly before attempting to move them.

6 Carefully loosen the baked brandy snaps from the baking sheet one at a time using a metal spatula.

7 Shape the brandy snaps into whatever shape you wish before leaving them to cool completely on a wire rack.

Shaping melted drop cookies

Melted drop cookies are pliable enough to be shaped into curls, rolls or baskets when they are warm. As they cool, the cookies become crisp and hard, retaining their shape.
Making curls Tuiles are usually curled after baking. They make a pretty decoration to any dessert. Remove the cookies from the oven, lift off the baking sheet and drape over a lightly oiled rolling pin, gently curling them around. Leave to cool and crisp before removing.
Making rolls These tightly rolled, wand-shaped cookies are great for serving as an accompaniment to any dessert. To make, remove from the oven and wind each cookie round a greased wooden spoon handle. Remove when firm. Cigarette Russes are a classic example of a rolled cookie.

Rolled cookies

A cookie dough that is rolled and cut may be a creamed, melted or rubbed-in mixture, but it must have the right consistency. If the dough is too dry it will crack and crumble; if it is too wet it may stick when rolling and spread during baking.

Simple almond cookies

The addition of almonds gives these cookies a delicious crunch.

MAKES 24

115g/4oz/¹/2 cup butter, softened
50g/2oz/¹/4 cup caster (superfine) sugar
1 egg, lightly beaten
15ml/1 tbsp ground almonds
200g/7oz/1³/4 cups plain
   (all-purpose) flour
30ml/2 tbsp cornflour (cornstarch)

1 Preheat the oven to 180°C/350°F/Gas 4. Lightly grease two baking sheets or line them with baking parchment. Beat the butter and sugar together until creamy. Gradually add the egg, beating well after each addition, then beat in the almonds. Sift over the flour and cornflour and mix to a soft dough.

2 Lightly knead the dough on a floured work surface for a few seconds, until smooth.

3 Shape the dough into a ball then flatten slightly into a round. Wrap in clear film (plastic wrap) and chill for about 30 minutes, or until firm but make sure it is not too stiff to roll.

4 On a floured work surface, roll out the dough lightly and evenly in one direction only to a thickness of about 3mm/¹/8in.

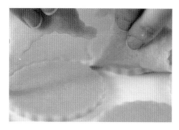

5 Stamp out 6.5cm/2¹/2in rounds using a fluted cookie cutter, or use another similar-sized shape. Gather up the scraps and re-roll the dough to make more cookies.

6 Transfer the cookies to the prepared baking sheets, leaving a space of at least 2.5cm/1in between each on the baking sheet. Chill for 30 minutes before baking.

7 Bake for 10 minutes until the cookies are a pale golden brown, making sure you rotate the baking sheets halfway through the cooking time. Remove from the oven and leave for 2–3 minutes. Transfer the cookies to a wire rack to cool.

ALL SHAPES AND SIZES

One of the greatest assets of rolled cookies is that they may be cut into any shape or size. There is a huge range of cutters available, but other ways of cutting and shaping cookies include using a pastry wheel or a knife, or even making your own template out of paper or card.

Using a knife or a pastry wheel to shape cookies

If you want to make squares, rectangles, triangles or bars, a sharp knife and a ruler are the perfect tools for the job. Instead of a knife, you could use a fluted pastry wheel to give an attractive edging. Roll out the dough to a square or rectangular shape, turning it frequently by 90 degrees. To make square cookies such as shortbread fingers, use a ruler to measure the dough so that it is rolled to the appropriate shape and size, then cut with a knife or pastry cutter.

Making a template

Sometimes you may want to create a more complex cookie shape for which you do not have a cutter. In this case you will need to make a template. It's probably best to avoid intricate designs, especially those with small protrusions as these may distort or burn during baking, and will break off easily once cooked.

Select the design, then draw on to a piece of thin cardboard or trace on to tracing paper first, then glue it on to cardboard. Place the template on the rolled out dough and hold firmly in place. Using a sharp knife, cut around the template to create the shape.

Making ring cookies

It can be difficult to transfer ring cookies to baking sheets without pulling them out of shape. One solution to this problem is to place rounds of dough on to the baking sheet, then cut out the centres with a smaller cutter. To make perfect rings, bake round cookies, then stamp out the centres while they are still warm.

Making multi-coloured rolled cookies

By using two or more different coloured doughs you can make a range of attractive cookies. The coloured doughs can be rolled, stamped out, then pieced together before baking, or the rolled doughs can be layered together then cut into cookie shapes.

Pinwheels

These cookies are made by rolling together two layers of different coloured dough.

1 Divide the cookie dough into two halves. Leave one half plain and flavour the other half by kneading in 15ml/1 tbsp sifted unsweetened cocoa powder and 5ml/1 tsp milk.

2 Wrap the cookie dough in clear film (plastic wrap) and then leave to chill in the refrigerator for at least 30 minutes.

3 Roll out each piece of cookie dough on a lightly floured work surface to a rectangle measuring 20 x 25cm/ 8 x 10in. Using a fine pastry brush, lightly brush the plain dough with lightly beaten egg white and place the coloured dough on top.

4 Roll the double-layered cookie dough up tightly from one of the long sides, then using a sharp knife, cut the dough into equal 5mm/¹⁄₄in thick slices.

Seven steps to success
• Always chill the dough in the refrigerator to firm it for at least 20 minutes and up to 1 hour before rolling. If you chill it for longer, leave it at room temperature for about 10 minutes before rolling out.
• Cookies should be rolled to a thickness of 3–5mm/¹⁄₈–¹⁄₄in.
• Use the minimum amount of flour when rolling out the dough. After cutting the cookies, brush off any excess flour with a clean, dry pastry brush.

• If the dough is sticky, even after chilling, roll it out between two sheets of baking parchment or clear film (plastic wrap).
• When stamping out the cookies, dip the cutter into flour, then press down firmly to cut right through the dough.
• Cut cookies closely together to minimize re-rolling scraps.
• If you haven't got a cutter, use a sharp knife or pastry wheel to cut the dough into squares or rectangles, or stamp out rounds using a thin-rimmed glass.

Piped cookies

For this type of cookie the mixture needs to be soft enough to pipe but firm enough to keep its shape during baking. Piped cookies are usually made by the creaming method, which gives them a crumbly, airy texture and makes blending in flavourings easy. Make sure that the butter is very soft before you start as this will make mixing and piping quick and easy.

Viennese piped cookies

With a little practice, these cookies can be piped into any shape you like.

MAKES 12

175g/6oz/³/4 cup unsalted (sweet) butter, softened

40g/1¹/2oz/3 tbsp icing (confectioners') sugar, sifted

2.5ml/¹/2 tsp vanilla extract

175g/6oz/1¹/2 cups plain (all-purpose) flour

40g/1¹/2oz/3 tbsp cornflour (cornstarch)

1 Preheat the oven to 180°C/350°F/ Gas 4. Grease two baking sheets or line with baking parchment.

2 Cream the butter and icing sugar together until pale and fluffy. Add the vanilla extract and beat for a few more seconds. Sift the flour and cornflour together over the butter mixture and mix until smooth.

3 Spoon the mixture into a piping (pastry) bag fitted with a large, star-shaped nozzle and pipe into the required shapes on the baking sheets. Make sure the shapes are spaced well apart.

4 Bake the cookies for 12 minutes, or until they are a pale golden colour. Leave for a few minutes on the baking sheets to firm up slightly before carefully transferring them to a wire rack to finish cooling.

PIPING SHAPES

Viennese cookie mixture can be piped into all manner of shapes and is very simple to make.

Viennese cookies

Round swirls are the classic shape for Viennese cookies. Spoon the mixture into a piping (pastry) bag fitted with a 1cm/¹/2in star nozzle. Pipe rosettes 5cm/2in across on to greased baking sheets, making sure to space them well apart.

Viennese whirls

Simply sandwich two Viennese cookies together using buttercream and a little sieved apricot jam for the filling.

Piped cookie variations

Once you have mastered making and piping the basic recipe, try adding flavourings to vary the cookie mixture.

Chocolate Substitute 30ml/2 tbsp unsweetened cocoa powder for the same quantity of flour.

Coffee Omit the vanilla extract and blend 5ml/1 tsp instant coffee powder with 5ml/1 tsp just boiled water. Cool, then add to the mixture with the flour.

Strawberry Use 40g/1¹/2oz/3 tbsp strawberry flavour blancmange powder instead of the cornflour.

Orange or lemon Beat the finely grated rind of half an orange or lemon into the creamed mixture.

Caramel To give the cookies a mild caramel flavour, use unrefined icing sugar.

Swiss fingers

Pretty piped fingers are very popular, and are very easy to make. Spoon the mixture into a piping bag fitted with a 1cm/1/2in star nozzle. Pipe 6cm/21/2in lengths on greased baking sheets, spacing well apart.

Oyster cookies

These pretty, sophisticated cookies resemble oyster shells. Spoon the mixture into a piping bag fitted with a 1cm/1/2in star nozzle and pipe about five lines to make shells. Make the shape wide at one end and tapered at the other.

OTHER PIPED COOKIES

Many other cookie mixtures are piped to give them an even length, width and shape. These cookies include langues de chats, filigree crowns and also Spanish churros (see overleaf for recipes).

Langues de chats

These classic French cookies are long, thin ovals with a slightly rough texture (like a cat's tongue).

MAKES 18

75g/3oz/6 tbsp unsalted (sweet)
    butter, softened
115g/4oz/1 cup icing (confectioners') sugar,
    sifted, plus extra for dusting
2 large (US extra large) egg whites
30ml/2 tbsp caster (superfine) sugar
75g/3oz/2/3 cup plain (all-purpose)
    flour, sifted

1 Preheat the oven to 200°C/400°F/ Gas 6. Grease or line two baking sheets. Cream the butter and icing sugar together until pale and fluffy.

2 In a separate bowl, whisk the egg whites to soft peaks, then add the caster sugar 15ml/1 tbsp at a time, whisking between each addition. Fold the whites into the butter mixture, then fold in the flour.

3 Spoon the mixture into a piping (pastry) bag fitted with a 1cm/1/2in plain nozzle and pipe 6cm/21/2in lengths on to the prepared baking sheets. Allow 5cm/2in between each cookie for spreading.

4 Bake for 5–7 minutes, or until the edges are lightly browned. Leave to cool on the baking sheets for 5 minutes before transferring to a wire rack to cool completely.

Perfect piping

To perfect your technique for making piped cookies, be sure to follow these four simple steps.

1 Drop the nozzle into the piping bag, pushing it down to fit firmly. Twist the nozzle end round so that there is a twist in the bag just above it.

2 Carefully push the twisted section of the bag inside the nozzle to ensure it is closed off.

3 Fold the top of the bag over your hand to make a "collar". Spoon in the mixture. When the bag is half full, gently twist the top to remove the air. Holding the top of the bag, push the mixture down.

4 Untwist the nozzle end of the bag. Hold the top of the bag firmly, using the other hand to guide the nozzle. Using firm, steady pressure, pipe the shape. Push down slightly then lift up.

Filigree crowns

These delicate, shaped cookies are made from finely piped lines of cookie mixture, which are first baked and then moulded into crowns. They make stunning little containers for desserts such as ice cream, mousse or fruit.

MAKES 6

1 egg white
50g/2oz/¼ cup caster
    (superfine) sugar
25g/1oz/¼ cup plain
    (all-purpose) flour

1 Preheat the oven to 200°C/400°F/ Gas 6. Draw six rectangles, each measuring about 20 x 7.5cm/8 x 3in, on six separate pieces of baking parchment. Place onto baking sheets.

2 Whisk the egg white and sugar together in a mixing bowl until foamy. Sift the flour over the egg mixture and stir in thoroughly.

3 Spoon the mixture into a piping (pastry) bag and snip off the tip to create a small hole. On each of the pieces of baking parchment, pipe thin wiggly lines from side to side to fill the marked shape, then pipe a little extra mixture down one of the long edges.

4 Bake the cookies for about 3 minutes. Remove the baking sheets from the oven and immediately roll the cookies around a straight-sided glass before they have a chance to cool.

5 Peel away the paper and stand the crowns upright. Remove the glass. If the mixture hardens before you've moulded the crowns, return it to the oven for a few seconds.

6 Leave to cool completely and store in an airtight container.

Spanish churros

These little Spanish cake-cookies are made from sweetened choux pastry, which is piped into hot oil and then deep-fried. They are delicious when sprinkled generously with cinnamon sugar.

MAKES 25

75g/3oz/6 tbsp butter, diced
250ml/8fl oz/1 cup water
115g/4oz/1 cup plain
    (all-purpose) flour
50g/2oz/4 tbsp caster
    (superfine) sugar
3 eggs, lightly beaten
2.5ml/½ tsp ground cinnamon

1 Heat the butter and water together in a small heavy pan until the butter has melted – do not allow the water to boil.

2 Lightly sift the plain flour and 15ml/1 tbsp of the caster sugar on to a large piece of baking parchment.

3 Once the butter has melted, bring to a boil, then add the flour and sugar. Remove the pan from the heat and beat the mixture vigorously. Cool for 5 minutes, then gradually beat in the eggs until the mixture is smooth and glossy.

4 Half-fill a large, heavy pan or deep-fryer with oil and heat to 190°C/375°F. Spoon the mixture into a piping (pastry) bag with a 1cm/½in star nozzle. Pipe five 10cm/4in lengths of the mixture into the hot oil being careful not to cause the fat to splash or spit. Fry the churros for 2 minutes, or until golden and crisp.

5 Remove from the oil with a slotted spoon and drain on kitchen paper. Repeat until all the mixture has been used. Mix the remaining caster sugar with the ground cinnamon and sprinkle over the churros. Serve warm.

Pressed cookies

Shaped cookies are amazingly simple to make using a commercial cookie press. The press comes with a range of patterned discs and may have several settings so that a variety of shapes and sizes of cookie can be made. Choose soft-textured cookie doughs that will easily push through the press.

Vanilla flowers

These pretty cookies use vanilla extract for an irresistible flavour.

MAKES 25

90g/3¹/₂oz/scant ¹/₂ cup
   butter, softened
90g/3¹/₂oz/¹/₂ cup caster
   (superfine) sugar
1 egg yolk
165g/5¹/₂oz/scant 1¹/₂ cups plain
   (all-purpose) flour
5ml/1 tsp milk
5ml/1 tsp vanilla extract

1 Cream the butter and sugar together until pale and fluffy. Beat in the egg yolk. Sift the flour over the butter mixture and then fold in with the milk and vanilla extract to make a soft dough. Knead for a few seconds until smooth.

2 Fill the cookie press cylinder almost to the top with the dough and then screw on the plunger. Press out the dough on to greased baking sheets, spacing the cookies well apart.

3 Chill the cookies for at least 30 minutes in the refrigerator. Decorate with sugar or nuts, if using. Meanwhile, preheat the oven to 180°C/350°F/Gas 4.

4 Bake in the oven for 15 minutes, or until very lightly browned. Leave to cool on the baking sheets for 5 minutes, then transfer to a wire rack to cool completely before serving.

Chocolate daisies

This dark chocolate mixture works perfectly in a cookie press.

MAKES 12

175g/6oz/³/₄ cup unsalted (sweet)
   butter, softened
40g/1¹/₂oz/3 tbsp icing (confectioners')
   sugar, sifted
175g/6oz/1¹/₂ cups plain
   (all-purpose) flour
25g/1oz/2 tbsp unsweetened cocoa powder
40g/1¹/₂oz/3 tbsp cornflour (cornstarch)

1 Preheat the oven to 180°C/ 350°F/Gas 4. Lightly grease two baking sheets or line them with baking parchment. Put the butter and icing sugar in a large bowl and cream together until very pale and fluffy.

2 Sift the flour, cocoa powder and cornflour together over the butter mixture and mix until smooth.

3 Put enough of the dough into the press to fill it almost to the top, then screw on the plunger.

4 Press out the dough on to the greased baking sheets. Make sure they are spaced well apart. Bake for about 12 minutes until just beginning to change colour. Leave the cookies for a few minutes on the baking sheets to firm up slightly before transferring them to a wire rack to cool completely.

Pressed cookie tips

• To achieve a short texture, cream the butter and sugar until very light and fold in the flour gently.
• The dough must be very smooth to go through the fine holes in the cookie discs, so don't add chunky ingredients, such as chopped nuts or chocolate chips.
• The dough must be sufficiently soft to be easily squeezed through the cookie press, but firm enough to hold its shape.
• If the mixture is too firm to press, add a few drops of milk.
• If the dough is slightly soft and sticks to the cookie disc, chill in the refrigerator for about 30 minutes until it has firmed up.
• Pressed cookies can be decorated with ingredients such as chocolate chips, sugar crystals or chopped nuts before baking.

Moulded cookies

Shaping cookie dough in a mould gives a professional finish. The dough can be either shaped in a mould, then turned out for baking or baked in the shaped tin itself. It is not essential to buy special moulds, you can improvise with plain tins for both shaping and baking.

SHAPING SHORTBREAD

Shortbread moulds usually have a carved design of a thistle and are available in different sizes. The mould should be brushed with a flavourless oil the first time it is used, then wiped with kitchen paper.

1 Make one quantity of shortbread mixture and roll out to a 15cm/6in round. Press it firmly into an 18cm/7in shortbread mould. Line a baking sheet with baking parchment.

2 Invert the mould on to the baking sheet, tapping the mould firmly to release the dough. Chill in the refrigerator for at least 30 minutes until firm.

3 Preheat the oven to 160°C/325°F/ Gas 3. Bake the shortbread for 35–40 minutes, or until pale golden. Sprinkle the top with a little caster (superfine) sugar, then leave to cool.

SHAPING MADELEINES

These French lemon cookies are baked in shell-shaped tins (pans).

MAKES 15

1 egg
65g/2¹/₂oz/generous ¹/₄ cup caster (superfine) sugar
65g/2¹/₂oz/9 tbsp self-raising (self-rising) flour
1.5ml/¹/₄ tsp baking powder
finely grated rind of ¹/₂ lemon
65g/2¹/₂oz/5 tbsp butter, melted and cooled

1 Preheat the oven to 220°C/425°F/ Gas 7. Brush the tins with melted unsalted (sweet) butter. Chill for 10 minutes, then brush lightly with butter again, dust with flour and shake off any excess.

2 Whisk the egg and sugar until thick and pale. Sift over half the flour with the baking powder and fold in the lemon rind. Pour half the remaining melted butter around the edge of the bowl and fold in gently.

3 Sift over the remaining flour. Pour in the rest of the melted butter around the edge of the bowl and fold in.

4 Spoon the mixture into the moulds, filling them just to the top. Bake for 10 minutes until golden. Leave for a few moments, then ease out with a metal spatula and transfer to a wire rack.

MAKING PETTICOAT TAILS

Shortbread is traditionally made into wedge-shaped petticoat tails.

1 Press one quantity of shortbread mixture into an 18cm/7in loose-based fluted flan tin (pan).

2 Prick the surface all over with a fork and then mark the shortbread into eight wedges using a sharp knife. If you do not have a fluted tin, use a straight-sided sandwich tin (layer pan) and press a pattern around the edge.

MAKING SQUARES AND BARS

Cookie dough can be baked in a loose-based square or rectangular tin (pan), then cut into pieces.

1 Press one quantity of shortbread mixture into a 15cm/6in square tin or two quantities into an 18 x 28cm/7 x 11in rectangular tin.

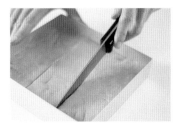

2 To cut into squares, make two cuts lengthways, then two cuts across for the square tin; four for the rectangular tin. For bars, cut in half lengthways, then cut across widthways.

SMALL MOULDED COOKIES

These can be made in tiny tartlet tins (muffin pans) or pretty metal chocolate moulds.

Press the shortbread dough into the prepared tins or moulds until level, then bake. Alternatively, turn out the moulded rounds on to greased or lined baking sheets. Chill before baking.

SHAPING COOKIES BY HAND

Classic hand-moulded cookies include jumbles, fork cookies and pretzels. Choose a cookie dough that will retain its shape when it is baked.

Fork cookies

These simple cookies are made by rolling dough into balls, then using a fork to make a pattern on the top.

MAKES 16

115g/4oz/¹/₂ cup butter, softened
50g/2oz/¹/₄ cup caster (superfine) sugar
150g/5oz/1¹/₄ cups self-raising (self-rising) flour, sifted

1 Preheat the oven to 180°C/350°F/ Gas 4. Lightly grease two baking sheets. Beat the butter in a bowl until creamy, then beat in the sugar. Stir in the flour and mix into a dough.

2 Shape into walnut-size balls and place on the baking sheets, spacing well apart. Dip a fork in cold water and use to flatten the cookies. Bake in the oven for about 10–12 minutes, or until the cookies are pale brown.

3 Leave the cookies to cool on the baking sheets for a few minutes, then carefully transfer to a wire rack to cool completely.

Pretzels

These are complicated shapes, so require a more pliable dough.

MAKES 40

115g/4oz/¹/₂ cup butter, softened
115g/4oz/1 cup icing (confectioners') sugar, sifted
1 egg, lightly beaten
15ml/1 tbsp golden (light corn) syrup
1.5ml/¹/₄ tsp vanilla extract
250g/9oz/2¹/₄ cups plain (all-purpose) flour, sifted

1 Preheat the oven to 190°C/375°F/ Gas 5. Beat the butter and sugar together until light and creamy. Beat in the egg, syrup and vanilla extract. Add the flour and stir to make a dough. Knead on a floured surface, then wrap and chill for 30 minutes.

2 Divide the dough into 40 pieces. Roll one piece into a thin strand about 25cm/10in long.

3 Create a loop with the strand, bring the ends together and press them into the top of the circle. Make the rest of the pretzels in the same way. Chill for 30 minutes.

4 Bake for 10 minutes until lightly browned, then cool on wire racks.

Bar cookies

These are a cross between a cake and a cookie; some are thin and crunchy, while others are thick and chewy or light and spongy.

Some bar cookies, such as brownies and flapjacks, are just a single layer, but many have two or more different layers that combine tastes and textures. Sometimes this base is partially or fully cooked first before the topping is added, then the oven temperature is lowered so that the topping doesn't overcook.

Always make bar cookies in the recommended tin (pan) size; even a small change in size will affect the cooking time and final result.

TOPPING IDEAS
There are dozens of different toppings for bar cookies. The base must be fairly firm but the topping can be softer, ranging from sponge cake to caramel, and from sticky meringue to chocolate. The following ideas are sufficient for an 18 x 28cm/7 x 11in tin (pan).

Coconut
This light topping has a delicate flavour and lovely texture. Beat two eggs, then stir in 115g/4oz/generous $1/2$ cup demerara (raw) sugar, 25g/1oz/3 tbsp ground rice, and 150g/5oz/$1^2/3$ cup desiccated (dry unsweetened shredded) coconut. Spread over the base and bake at 180°C/350°F/Gas 4 for 25 minutes.

Crumble or streusel
This works best on top of a slightly soft or sticky base or filling such as jam, fruit purée or soft caramel.

Beat 115g/4oz/$1/2$ cup butter until creamy, then mix in 50g/2oz/$1/4$ cup soft light brown sugar. Stir in 115g/4oz/$2/3$ cup semolina and 115g/4oz/1 cup plain wholemeal (whole-wheat) flour until the mixture resembles breadcrumbs. Add 2.5ml/$1/2$ tsp ground ginger. Sprinkle over the base and press down. Bake at 160°C/325°F/Gas 3 for about 40 minutes.

Chocolate
This topping is incredibly simple to make and produces great results.

Chop 350g/12oz plain (semisweet), milk or white chocolate. Sprinkle the chocolate over the hot cookie base, then return the base to the oven for 1 minute until melted. Mark into bars when the chocolate is almost set.

Citrus cheesecake
To make this zesty topping, put the finely grated rind of two lemons and two limes in a bowl with 225g/8oz/1 cup melted butter, 30ml/2 tbsp caster (superfine) sugar and three eggs. Whisk until the mixture is thick and mousse-like.

Sift over 40g/1$1/2$oz/$1/3$ cup plain (all-purpose) flour and 2.5ml/$1/2$ tsp baking powder and fold in with 30ml/2 tbsp lemon or lime juice. Pour over the cookie base and bake in the oven at 180°C/350°F/Gas 4 for about 25 minutes.

Meringue
This produces a wonderfully light, topping that melts in the mouth.

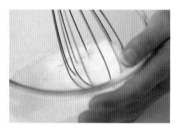

Whisk two egg whites with a pinch of salt in a bowl until they form soft peaks. Gradually whisk in 115g/4oz/generous $1/2$ cup caster (superfine) sugar, a spoonful at a time, until the mixture becomes stiff and glossy.

Fold into the mixture 2.5ml/$1/2$ tsp cornflour (cornstarch) and 5ml/1 tsp lemon juice. Spread over the cookie base and swirl with a metal spatula to form soft peaks. Bake at 140°C/275°F/Gas 1 for about 40 minutes until the meringue is set and tinged golden brown.

Nut caramel

Put 175g/6oz/²/₃ cup soft light brown sugar, 30ml/2 tbsp golden (light corn) syrup and 175g/6oz/³/₄ cup butter in a pan. Heat gently until the sugar has dissolved, then bring to the boil and simmer for 5 minutes, until a rich golden colour. Stir in 175g/6oz/1 cup chopped roasted unsalted peanuts. Immediately spread over base and leave to cool.

BAKING THE PERFECT BROWNIE

Brownies, named after their dark rich colour, should be quite moist and chewy; with a sugary crust on the outside, but soft and squidgy on the inside.

There are many different recipes for brownies, all varying in richness. Plainer ones rely on unsweetened cocoa powder alone, while others use vast quantities of melted chocolate. Often, a small amount of coffee is added. This is barely perceptible to the taste, but cuts through the sweetness a little.

True brownies have an extremely high proportion of sugar and fat and most contain nuts, usually walnuts or pecan nuts.

Lighter versions and brownies made from white chocolate are often referred to as blondies.

It is very important to remove brownies from the oven as soon as the cooking time is up, even though they will still seem quite soft. They will soon firm up on standing and, if overcooked, the characteristic gooey texture will be ruined.

Classic chocolate brownies

Richly coloured and flavoured, these are deliciously gooey and moist.

MAKES 24

225g/8oz plain (semisweet) chocolate
225g/8oz/1 cup butter, diced
3 eggs
225g/8oz/generous 1 cup caster (superfine) sugar
30ml/2 tbsp strong black coffee
75g/3oz/²/₃ cup self-raising (self-rising) flour
pinch of salt
150g/5oz/1¹/₄ cups chopped walnuts
5ml/1 tsp vanilla extract

1 Preheat the oven to 180°C/375°F/ Gas 5. Grease and line a 18 x 28cm/ 7 x 11in tin (pan). Break the chocolate into squares and place in a heatproof bowl with the butter. Set the bowl over a pan of barely simmering water and leave for 5–10 minutes, stirring occasionally until the mixture is melted and smooth. Remove the bowl from the pan and leave to cool for 5 minutes.

2 In a large bowl, beat the eggs, sugar and coffee until smooth, then gradually beat in the cooled melted chocolate mixture.

3 Sift the flour and salt over the mixture, then fold in together with the walnuts and vanilla extract.

4 Spoon the mixture into the prepared tin and bake for about 35 minutes, or until just firm to the touch in the centre. (Don't bake it for any longer than this as the mixture will still be soft under the crust, but will firm up as it cools. Overcooking gives a dry result.)

5 Leave the brownies to cool in the tin then turn out on to a board, trim off the crusty edges and cut into squares using a serrated knife and a gentle sawing action.

Baking cookies

To ensure perfect cookies every time, you must take as much care with cooking them as you did with the mixing and shaping of the dough.

USING THE OVEN

Always allow time to preheat the oven; it will take about 15 minutes to reach the required temperature (although fan-assisted ovens may heat more quickly).

Unless the recipe instructs otherwise, bake cookies in the middle, or just above the middle, of the oven. If you are baking large quantities of cookies, do not put more than two baking sheets in the oven at once because this can cause the oven temperature to drop. This particularly applies to cookies that have been chilled beforehand.

USING BAKING SHEETS

If you are using a new baking sheet, check that it fits into the oven before you arrange the cookies on it; ideally, there should be a small gap at either side and at the back of the baking sheet to allow hot air to circulate. If you need to divide the cookies between two or more baking sheets, put the same number of cookies on each sheet, so the batches cook at the same rate.

If you put two baking sheets of cookies in the oven at the same time, switch them around halfway through the cooking time. If you need to cook a second batch of cookies straight away, let the baking sheet cool before placing the next batch of raw cookies on it; a hot baking sheet might make the raw cookies spread, which will result in thin, irregular-sized cookies.

TIME AND TEMPERATURE

Baking times may vary slightly with different ovens, and can depend on how chilled the cookies were when cooking commenced. Get to know your oven. If you feel that it is either too cool or too hot, use an oven thermometer to check the temperature. If it needs adjusting, change your oven temperature dial accordingly to correct this.

Always check cookies a few minutes before the end of the suggested cooking time. Unlike cakes, they will not loose volume or sink if the oven door is opened, although you should avoid doing this too frequently or the temperature will drop and the cookies will be less crisp. Second and subsequent batches of cookies may take slightly less time to cook.

COOKING GUIDELINES

Not all cookies are the same. Different types of cookie need to be cooked in different ways and at different temperatures.

Drop cookies

These are baked in a moderate oven, around 180°C/350°F/Gas 4. This gives them a chance to spread out a little before they set. To make cookies that are crisp on the outside, but with a slightly soft and chewy centre, remove from the oven as soon as the edges are dark golden but the middle is still a little pale. For crisp cookies, wait until the whole cookie is lightly browned before removing from the oven. To achieve an even crisper result, spread out the mixture slightly to make a thinner layer before baking.

Rolled, piped and pressed cookies

These types of cookies are usually chilled for at least 30 minutes before baking to prevent them spreading too much during cooking. They are cooked in a moderate to hot oven, between 180°C/350°F/Gas 4 and 200°C/400°F/Gas 6.

1 Place the cookies on a baking sheet, then chill for 30 minutes.

2 Bake until pale golden; do not allow to colour too much. Leave to cool slightly on the baking sheets, then carefully transfer to wire racks to cool completely before serving.

Refrigerator cookies

These cookies have a relatively high fat content and so are baked at a moderately high temperature, around 190°C/375°F/Gas 5.

1 Slice the chilled cookie mixture and arrange on ungreased baking sheets, spaced evenly apart. Do not use non-stick sheets or line the sheets with baking parchment because this will make the cookies spread out during baking.

2 The cookies must be well chilled before baking, so either cook them as soon as they have been sliced or place the baking sheets in the refrigerator until ready to bake.

Bar cookies

This type of cookie is usually baked in a moderately low to moderate oven, between 160°C/325°F/Gas 3 and 180°C/350°F/Gas 4.

1 Bar cookies that have a shortbread, pastry or crumb base are often partially baked in the oven before the topping is added afterwards. This process allows the cookie base to be cooked through until crisp and firm without the topping becoming overcooked.

2 To test whether sponge or brownie mixtures are cooked, insert a skewer or cocktail stick (toothpick) into the middle of the mixture. It should come out clean. If it doesn't then return to the oven to cook for a further few minutes.

COOLING COOKIES

Always make sure to follow the instructions in the recipe when cooling cookies. Most cookies are quite delicate and so will benefit from being left on the baking sheets for a minute or two to firm up, before removing to a wire rack to cool completely.

Always use a thin metal spatula to transfer cookies to wire racks. Placing them on a wire rack allows the air to circulate around them, and prevents any moisture being trapped, which can make them lose their crisp texture.

Don't be tempted to try to cram too many cookies on the rack at any one time and avoid placing very hot cookies on top of each other; this will cause them to lose their crispness.

Cookies such as tuiles and brandy snaps that are to be moulded into different shapes should be removed from the baking sheets after 30 seconds. Others such as bar cookies may benefit from being allowed to cool in the baking tins (pans). Placing the whole tin on a wire rack can speed the cooling.

Baking cookies at high altitude

Above 3,000m/9,800ft above sea level, atmospheric pressure becomes lower, which makes liquid boil faster and so slightly more liquid and less raising agents are necessary. Reducing fat and increasing the quantity of flour can also help.

ALTITUDE	3,000m/9,800ft	5,000m/16,350ft	7,000m/22,900ft
Sugar For each 115g/4oz/ generous $^1/_2$ cup, reduce by:	10ml/2 tsp	115ml/1 tbsp	30ml/2 tbsp
Baking powder For each 5ml/1 tsp, reduce by:	0.75ml/$^1/_8$ tsp	1.5ml/$^1/_4$ tsp	1.5ml/$^1/_4$ tsp
Liquid For each 75ml/5 tbsp, increase by:	5ml/1 tsp	10ml/2 tsp	30ml/2 tbsp
Oven temperature Increase by:	5°C/10°F/Gas $^1/_4$	15°C/25°F/Gas $^1/_2$	20°C/35°F/Gas 1$^1/_2$

Cookie decoration

Decorating cookies can add the final flourish to home-made cookies and can be one of the most enjoyable aspects of cookie-making. Cookies can be decorated before baking, while the cookies are still warm from the oven, or when they are completely cool.

DECORATING COOKIES BEFORE BAKING
Techniques for decorating unbaked cookies can range from the most simple sprinkling of sugar or nuts to brushing with a glossy glaze or painting intricate designs with edible food colouring.

Sugar
A crunchy sugar topping is one of the easiest and most effective ways to decorate unbaked cookies. Many different sugars can be used. Caster (superfine) sugar can be sprinkled straight over raw cookies to give a subtle, crunchy texture. Coarse sugars such as demerara (raw)

sugar and irregular-shaped coffee crystals give a crunchier result. Pretty coloured sugars and crushed white and brown sugar lumps can also produce a lovely effect when sprinkled over raw cookies.

Moist cookie doughs can simply be sprinkled with sugar, while drier cookies such as refrigerator or rolled cookies may benefit from being lightly brushed with a little water or milk before they are sprinkled with sugar.

Nuts
Chopped and flaked (sliced) nuts can be sprinkled over cookies in the same way as sugar. Nuts brown during baking, so avoid using on cookies that are baked at a high temperature or on cookies that are baked for a long time as the nuts may overcook.

A whole nut can be pressed into the top of each individual cookie. (This technique is best suited to soft cookie doughs.) The nuts may be purely decorative, or they can be used to indicate the type of cookie. For example, you might want to press a whole hazelnut into a hazelnut cookie, or an almond into an almond flavoured cookie.

Glazes
Brushing a glaze over cookies can serve two purposes, either to provide a sticky surface that nuts or sugar can stick to, or to give an attractive finish. To give cookies a rich, glossy finish, use a whole beaten egg or yolk. Brush the glaze lightly on the top, without it dripping over the edges. Lightly beaten egg white produces a clear, shiny finish. Brush over the cookies halfway through the baking time, so that it soaks into the cookies slightly and does not set to a crackled glaze. It looks very effective sprinkled with a little sugar.

Painted cookies
Edible food colouring can be painted directly on to unbaked cookies to make pretty decorative patterns. This technique, however, is best suited to drier, firmer cookie doughs such as rolled and refrigerator cookies.

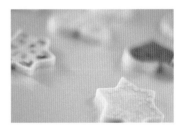

To decorate cookies, cut the dough into shapes, place them on baking sheets and chill for 30 minutes. Beat an egg yolk and mix in a few drops of food colouring. Using a very fine paintbrush, paint patterns on to the cookies, and then bake. (Remember that the yellow egg yolk may affect the colour of the food colouring.)

DECORATING COOKIES AFTER BAKING

As with unbaked cookies, you can transform simple baked cookies into something special with just a few easy decorating techniques. A sprinkling of sugar takes just a few seconds, while dusting a design using a stencil or writing a message with a food colouring pen takes only a little longer.

Decorating cookies with sugar

Different types of sugar can be used to give a range of effects on various baked cookies.

Icing/confectioners' sugar A dusting of icing sugar gives plain cookies a professional finish and is a useful way of disguising any imperfections. Use a fine sieve or sugar dredger to give an even coating.

Caster/superfine sugar Simply sprinkling freshly baked cookies with a little caster (superfine) sugar is perhaps one of the quickest and easiest decorations to use. Sprinkle sugar over while they are still warm so that the sugar sticks to the cookies. Coarse-grained sugars Granulated and demerara (raw) sugar look pretty sprinkled over cookies but, because the grains are so large, they will not

stick to the cookie on their own. The easiest way to overcome this problem is to use a glaze suchas beaten egg white to stick the sugar to the cookie, then return the cookies to the oven to bake for 2–3 minutes.

Cookies such as sweet pretzels are usually coated with demerara sugar, then grilled (broiled) until the sugar starts to caramelize.

Decorating cookies with sugar glazes

Cookies such as Lebkuchen are sometimes given a shiny finish with a sugar glaze. These glazes may be clear or opaque and are brushed over cookies while they are still warm.

Lebkuchen glaze This semi-opaque glaze gently softens the surface of the cookie, giving it a chewy texture. Sift 175g/6oz/1 1/2 cups icing (confectioners') sugar into a bowl. Add 2.5ml/1/2 tsp almond extract, 5ml/1 tsp lemon juice and 30ml/2 tbsp hot water. Mix together until smooth, then brush over the hot Lebkuchen and cool.

Clear glaze This simple glaze gives cookies a glossy finish. Heat 25g/1oz/2 tbsp sugar in 60ml/4 tbsp water until the sugar dissolves. Boil rapidly for 5 minutes, or until reduced by half.

Leave to cool. Gradually beat in 115g/4oz/1 cup sifted icing sugar, then brush over warm cookies and leave to set.

Stencilling designs

This is an easy way to decorate cookies. You can buy stencils that are specially made for cake and cookie decorating, or you can make your own by drawing a small design on thin cardboard and cutting it out. Make sure there is a contrast between the colour of the cookie and the dusting ingredient; for example, icing sugar works well on chocolate cookies, while unsweetened cocoa powder is better on paler coloured cookies.

Food-colouring pens

These pens look like felt-tipped pens but they are filled with edible food colouring. They come in a range of colours from primary to pastels and some are flavoured.

They can be used directly on to the cookies or on to the icing and are most effective on rolled cookies; icing must be dry and firm. Use the decorating pens in the same way as an ordinary pen. Draw designs, write messages, or colour in shapes.

ICING COOKIES

Cookies can look lovely decorated with pretty coloured icing. It is important to get the consistency of icing right; too thick and it will be difficult to spread; too thin and it will run off the edges and soak into the cookie.

There are many different types of icing that can be used to decorate cookies and they can range in colour from the palest pastels to vibrant primary colours. Glacé or fondant icings give a smooth, glossy finish and can be used to create simple finishing touches to the cookies, while royal icing can be swirled to give a textured pattern or piped into delicate and intricate designs. Whatever type of icing you use, iced cookies should usually be eaten within 3 or 4 days.

Glacé icing

This is the simplest type of icing to make and use. It is perfect for drizzling and piping simple designs.

TO COVER 24 COOKIES

115g/4oz/1 cup icing
  (confectioners') sugar
a few drops of vanilla extract (optional)
15ml/1 tbsp hot water
a few drops of food colouring (optional)

Lightly sift the icing sugar into a large bowl, then add the vanilla extract, if using. Gradually stir in the hot water until the mixture is the consistency of thick cream. Add the food colouring, and continue stirring until smooth.

Top coating This is the simplest technique. Spoon a little icing on to the centre of the cookie, then carefully spread it out almost to the edges using the back of the spoon.

Feathered glacé icing Spoon a little icing over a cookie to cover it, then pipe several thin, straight parallel lines of icing in a contrasting colour across the top of the cookie.

Starting at the middle of the cookie, draw a wooden cocktail stick (toothpick) through the lines in the opposite direction, gently dragging the colour through the icing and creating a feathered effect.

Drizzled icing Place the cooled cookies on a wire rack. Using a paper piping (pastry) bag or teaspoon, carefully drizzle fine lines of icing over the tops of the cookies. You can then drizzle more icing at right angles to these first lines, if you want a more decorative pattern.

Cobweb icing Cover a cookie in icing, then pipe on fine, concentric circles of icing in a contrasting colour, starting from the centre and working outwards. Draw a cocktail stick (toothpick) from the centre of the cookie to the outside edge, dividing the cookie into quarters, then repeat to divide it into eighths.

Royal icing

This icing sets hard to give a good finish so is perfect for piping designs and messages on cookies such as gingerbread.

TO COVER 30 COOKIES

1 egg white, at room temperature or
  7.5ml/1¹/₂ tsp albumen powder
225g/8oz/2 cups icing (confectioners'
  sugar, sifted, plus extra if necessary

Beat the egg white in a medium bowl for a few seconds with a fork. (If using albumen powder, mix according to the instructions.) Mix in the icing sugar a little at a time until the mixture stands in soft peaks and is thick enough to spread. If the icing is for piping, beat in a little more icing sugar until the icing will stand in stiff peaks. Carefully spread or pipe the icing over the cookies. Leave to set before serving.

DECORATING COOKIES WITH CHOCOLATE

The taste, texture and versatility of chocolate makes it one of the most popular ingredients for decorating cookies. It can be used to coat cookies, pipe or drizzle patterns, or even write short messages.

Melting chocolate

For most decorating techniques, chocolate needs to be melted. Take care doing this as overheating will spoil both the texture and flavour. When melting chocolate, choose a variety with a high proportion of cocoa butter as this will melt more smoothly.

Using a double boiler Break the chocolate into pieces and put in the top of a double boiler or in a heatproof bowl set over a pan of hot water; the water should not touch the top container. Bring the water to simmering point, then reduce heat to a gentle simmer.

Check every few minutes, turning off the heat if necessary. Stir once or twice until the chocolate is smooth.

Using a microwave This is a quick way of melting chocolate. Break the chocolate into pieces and place in a microwave-safe bowl. Melt in bursts of 30–60 seconds, checking often and reducing the time as the chocolate begins to soften. Stop microwaving before all the chocolate has melted and stir.

Using direct heat This is only suitable for recipes where chocolate is melted with milk or butter.

Put the liquid ingredients in the pan, add the chocolate and then melt over a low heat. When the chocolate starts to melt, turn off the heat and keep stirring until the mixture is smooth.

Using melted chocolate

When you are decorating cookies with melted chocolate, handle the chocolate as little as possible and use a metal spatula to lift and move the decorated cookies around. Always leave to set at room temperature and do not store in the refrigerator unless the weather is exceptionally warm.

Coating cookies with chocolate Before coating cookies in melted chocolate, make sure that it is just starting to cool; chocolate that is hot or even very warm will soak into the cookies and spoil their texture.

Dipping cookies in chocolate Round or shaped cookies are often half-coated in chocolate and finger cookies sometimes have one or both ends dipped in chocolate. This method is simpler than completely covering cookies in chocolate.

If you're planning to sandwich cookies together, they are best dipped in chocolate before filling as the warmth of the chocolate may melt the filling.

Piping chocolate Use a paper piping (pastry) bag with the end snipped off to pipe thin lines of chocolate.

Place cookies on a sheet of baking parchment and pipe over thin lines.

Colouring white chocolate You also can colour melted white chocolate with cake decorator's colouring dust (petal dust). Do not use liquid or paste food colourings as these will spoil the texture of the chocolate.

Storing cookies

With few exceptions, cookies are best eaten on the day that they are made. Some such as American-style soft cookies are delicious when still warm from the oven, but most cookies need to be cooled first to allow them to crisp. If you're not planning to eat them straight away, store them as soon as they have cooled. This will prevent crisp cookies from becoming soft and soft ones from drying out. Store crisp and soft cookies separately.

SOFT COOKIES

It is essential to keep these cookies in an airtight container and, if possible, they should also be stored in the refrigerator to retain the freshly baked flavour.

Carefully pack cookies into an airtight container and seal. If the lid of the container isn't tight-fitting, put the cookies inside a plastic bag first. To restore the texture of soft cookies that have hardened add a slice of brown bread to the container. Replace the bread daily.

CRISP COOKIES

The container for this type of cookie does not need to be absolutely airtight; unless the atmosphere is very humid, a slight flow of air will help them stay crisp. Glass jars and ceramic containers with cork stoppers are ideal for storing crisp cookies.

Place a little crumpled tissue paper in the base of the jar to help absorb any moisture. If cookies become soft, place them on a baking sheet and put in a preheated oven at 150°C/300°F/Gas 2 for about 3 minutes to re-crisp. Remove and cool on a wire rack before storing.

COOKIES IN THE FREEZER

Undecorated baked cookies can be frozen successfully. Freeze the cookies on trays, then pack into an airtight container interleaving with baking parchment. (Avoid freezing cream-filled cookies such as brandy snaps as these will quickly become soggy.) To thaw cookies, leave at room temperature for about 20 minutes.

Iced cookies can also be frozen in the same way, but they should be removed from the airtight container and thawed on a wire rack. The icing may be spoilt if they thaw in layers.

CHILLING AND FREEZING COOKIE DOUGH

As long as cookie dough doesn't contain leavening ingredients, it can be stored in the refrigerator overnight or, in some cases, for up to a week.

Cookie dough can be frozen for up to 3 months but the flavours lose their intensity after a month. For optimum results, the dough is best frozen for just a few weeks.

To store cookie dough in the refrigerator, wrap it tightly in a piece of clear film (plastic wrap) or place it in a bowl and cover it tightly with clear film.

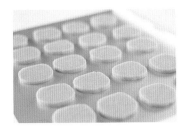

To freeze, wrap the dough in a double layer of clear film, then store in an airtight container.

To freeze unbaked cookies, open-freeze them on trays, then pack into airtight containers, interleaving them with layers of baking parchment.

WHAT WENT WRONG AND WHY

Occasionally cookies don't turn out quite as you had hoped. If you have a problem when baking, try to work out why so that you can either remedy it at the time, or at least avoid it next time you bake cookies.

Problem	Cause	Remedy
The dough is very soft and won't hold its shape.	Too much liquid or fat or too little flour, or the dough has become too warm.	Always measure ingredients carefully. Chill the dough for 30 minutes before baking. If it is still too soft, work in a little extra flour.
The dough is dry and crumbly and won't hold together.	Not enough liquid or fat or too much flour, or the dough may not have been kneaded sufficiently.	Try gently kneading the dough; the warmth of your hands may bring it together. If the dough includes egg, check the right size was used. Knead in a little beaten egg, milk or soft butter.
The cookies are not evenly cooked.	The cookies are either of uneven sizes on the baking sheet; or some cookies were placed too near the edge of the sheet.	Make sure that all the cookies on a baking sheet are an even size. Leave at least a 2.5cm/1in gap around the edge of the baking sheet and turn the sheets around halfway through baking.
The cookies stick to the baking sheet.	The baking sheet was not greased or was greased unevenly. Alternatively, it may have been greased with salted butter.	Use melted, unsalted (sweet) butter or oil for greasing or line the sheet with baking parchment.
The cookies crumble when removed from baking sheet.	Cookies that have a very high butter content are often more fragile than less rich ones.	Leave fragile cookies to cool on the baking sheet for at least 3 minutes before transferring to a wire rack.
The cookies are dry and too crisp on top.	The oven was too hot or the cookies were baked for too long.	If you have concerns about the temperature of your oven, use an oven thermometer. Check cookies a few minutes before end of cooking time.
The cookies spread out too much on the baking sheet.	The cookies were not chilled before baking, or, the baking sheet was over-greased when the cookies were added.	Most cookies benefit from chilling before baking. Grease baking sheets only lightly. Some cookies such as refrigerator cookies should be baked on ungreased baking sheets. Always use cold baking sheets.
The cookies are burnt on the base but not on the top.	There are a number of possible causes: baking too low down in the oven, or at too low a temperature; the baking sheets may be poor quality, or you may have used salted butter for greasing.	Check the oven temperature and bake cookies on the middle shelf. Avoid thin or very dark baking sheets. Butter burns at a lower temperature, so use oil for cookies baked at high temperatures or for a long time.

Index